William Johnston Hutchinson

The Poems of William Johnston Hutchinson

Second Edition

William Johnston Hutchinson

The Poems of William Johnston Hutchinson
Second Edition

ISBN/EAN: 9783744711098

Printed in Europe, USA, Canada, Australia, Japan

Cover: Foto ©Thomas Meinert / pixelio.de

More available books at **www.hansebooks.com**

THE

POEMS

OF

WILLIAM JOHNSTON HUTCHINSON.

[SECOND EDITION.]

NEW YORK:
1878.

Entered according to Act of Congress, in the year 1876,
By WILLIAM JOHNSTON HUTCHINSON,
In the Office of the Librarian of Congress at Washington.

EVENING POST PRESSES.

My Cousin Clara,

THIS VOLUME IS INSCRIBED

PREFATORY NOTE.

Many of the following Poems have gone abroad through the courtesy of the Press.

Sometime since, that the flavor of the beverage might be intimated, before venturing to pour it out more liberally, a small Edition of the Poems was distributed among the friends of the Author.

In its maturer form, this volume is submitted to the reading public.

W. J. H.

NEW YORK, January, 1878.

CONTENTS.

Alcibiades' Soliloquy	97
Antony's Lament over Cæsar	47
Alone	51
Asleep	72
Along the Stream	80
Ayesha	102
Arsinoe	168
Althæa and Marigold	213
A Thoughtless, Bitter Word	144
A Trifle it was, as Light as the Air	178
Autumn Musings	33
At Moments in the Month of Many Roses	14
Berenece	105
Belated	139
Bedouin Robber and Steed	150
Canst Thou Forget?	119
Down where the Sea and Rivers Meet	44
Deus! Meus!	56
Death of Julian Chlorus	68
David and Absalom	156
Echo	100
Ethel	106
Epigram	173
Exquisite Draperies Hanging in the West	203

CONTENTS.

En Gascogne	31
Faltering	186
Golden Hours	162
Hollywood	73
Hymn	211
Invitation to Æneas	121
In Remembrance	142
Invocation to Polhymnia	217
I am Dying, Egypt, Dying	206
I Watched Upon a Point of Beaten Sand	22
La Fleur	124
Lines to the Alabama River	125
Lines: The Sense of Death	218
Little Maid of Anglesey	128
Love's Index	148
Lily of the Valley	164
Lake and Wild Fowl	224
Lines: Minstrel, Stay	227
Lines to ——	23
My Argosies	61
Motherless	67
Messages	82
My Mate and I	180
Marjorie	145
On Concluding Cicero	108
On Concluding Gibbon's History	108
Ode: Horace; On Contentment	191
Ode: Horace; To Thaliarchus	194
Ode: Horace; To Quintus Dellius	195

CONTENTS.

ODE: HORACE; TO LICINIUS MURENA	197
ODE: HORACE; TO GROSPHUS	201
ODE: HORACE; ON HIS OWN WORKS	205
ODE: HORACE; CIVIL WAR	209
OUT ON THE MYSTIC SEA	199
O, FLY THOSE MUSIC-BREATHING HALLS!	146
ON THE SANDS	9
PAUSANIAS	109
PSALM CXXVI	12
RUSSIAN HYMN	24
SONNET: TO MY SISTER	137
SONNET: JANUARY	214
SONNET: TO ———, WITH THE ODES OF PINDAR	216
SONNET: TO EDNA	155
SONNET: THERE IS AN ATTRIBUTE	166
SONNET: WHEN ON MY BRIEF EXISTENCE	171
SONNET: COME, DOUBTER	174
SONNET: MINE EARS DRINK IN	175
SONNET: TO JULIA	177
SONNET: AND HAD I PLANNED	187
SONNET: THE ASSYRIAN MONARCH	188
SONNET: THE SUNBURST	208
SONNET: TO MILDRED	8
SUNSHINE IN WINTER	160
SONG: KNIGHT OF THE TWELFTH CENTURY	219
STRIKE, STRIKE THE HARP!	17
THE PILGRIM	1
THE LANGUAGE OF THE SEA	38
THE EVENING WALK	40

CONTENTS.

The Invitation.	42
The Lost Treasure	52
The Revellers	58
The Wager	63
The Fortunate Isles of the Bless'd	65
The Sacrilege of Alaric	75
The Pledge	79
The Fog-Bell	86
The Death of the Oriole	88
The Cape of Storms	91
The Recluse	93
The Twilight Hour	123
The Complaint	127
The Failure	132
The Star of Friendship	138
The Changing of the Tides	140
The Watcher	152
The Matins Bell	172
The Burial of Pizarro	182
The Dreamers	189
The Hours	204
The Battler	220
The Battle-Field	225
To the Robin	41
To My Sister	46
To a Friend	59
To Philomel	103
To Brother	130
To Mysie	167

CONTENTS.

To a Sunbeam	176
Theodora	89
Tell Me, Good Lady-Mother, Why	135
The Succession of Spring	6
The Succession of Summer	13
The Succession of Autumn	28
The Succession of Winter	36
To a Sleeping Child	29
The Muezzin	25
Unreconciled	215
Venus is again the Evening Star	37
Would Day were Come	55
We Watch the Dawning of Her Life	15
When Thou Art Gone	18
When I am Lowly Laid to Rest	20

POEMS.

THE PILGRIM.

ARGUMENT.

A would-be pilgrim leaves his humble home, and is by inspiration led to a mountain top. He sees the fair earth spread before him ; and, reading its history as in a picture, becomes unwilling to mingle in such scenes. Saddened by the character of man as there depicted, but soothed by Nature's charms and lovely examples, he retraces his steps irresolutely homeward.

EHOLD a toil-stained pilgrim leave
    his cot,
Resolved to shun forever his hard lot ;
And speed, with quickening steps, forth
    from the vale
That hears the roar, but 'scapes the
    wintry gale,
On toward the mountain's base ; nor feel the darts
That flaming downward come. Nay ! it imparts

A new-born vigor to his feet : he'd gain
Yon mountain top while daylight's charms yet
    reign.

Upward he pants. There, dimly in the skies,
He sees the rock toward which his wistful eyes
A thousand times in boyhood's years have
    turned,
And kindled in his breast the fire that burned
Through all the weary, seeming endless years ;
Nor ceased to smoulder, though a flood of tears
Had there its angry surges vainly rolled
To stay the flame he fain would have controlled.

Thus doth he climb the chamois' rocky track,
Nor stays an instant to look quickly back ;
For not until he gains yon dizzy height
Would he desire to view the wondrous sight :
Then, then, in one intoxicating draught,
Its pleasing aspects may be deeply quafft.
Chasms may yawn and towering crags may mock,
What cares he now ? his feet have gained the
    rock ;
And, with a wistful cry, to view the world
He lifts his eyes—and, lo ! it lies unfurled
In one long pageant, one unbounded page,
As told in words and verse from age to age.

His eyes seek first the spot where man drew
    breath,
And tell his heart how quickly man courts death ;
Not on himself the load of ruin bears,
But bows his kind through all the course of
    years.
He sees the lands with peoples multiplied ;
He sees the arm that placed them there defied ;
He hears His servant plead ; no longer urge,
But dreadful silence reigns ; the boisterous surge
Sweeps down o'er all. Fair Nature's dark'ning
    face
Hath not a smile for one of all that race.

    He looks again, and other nations rise
On Asia's plains, 'neath Egypt's cloudless skies.
Uncounted hosts in glittering war's array
Make death their trade—a monarch's voice obey
To spoil a peaceful land, or ruthless sweep
With deeds of blood that make bright angels
    weep ;
And they, in turn, a satrap's chain to feel,
Sesostris' line crushed 'neath the Persian's wheel ;
They then to yield to crushing conquest's blight,
And feel with Athens Macedonia's might
For one dire instant—then to cast their charms
Without one cry to Roma's conquering arms.

On come the ages. Now a ruthless host
Steals from its barren home, stern Scythia's coast,
With dread destruction loosened in its train—
Each home to sack, each palace deeply stain;
And nearer yet,—when Christian nations rise
With History's page to teach them to despise
Such fearful arts,—yet ever will pursue
With fiendish cries war's way, and still renew
The senseless struggle that with glory crowned
Fair Fortune's guests, while woes their millions drowned.

But now he turns from mankind's endless crimes,
And views with swelling joy the beauteous climes
That picture all the earth. Majestic forms arise,
Of sombre hue; but, as they pierce the skies,
Reflecting gems flash back the rays of fire,
And bathe his soul in transports of desire.
The grand old Ocean, breaking on the shore,
The old, old tale, repeating o'er and o'er
Of secrets kept deep down within its breast;
Of forms held dear, forever laid to rest;
Of some fair island, laved by summer seas,
Where sea-nymphs' tresses flutter in the breeze.—

The distant river, silver-sparkling thread,
Brings quick delight, as swiftly in its bed
It pours along with ceaseless, noiseless motion
To pay its tribute to unbounded ocean.
Doth it not teach of life ?   A joyous thing
It seeks the light—'tis then a feeble spring,
But downward seeks its course, and grows
    apace,
And in an hour enters for the race
A genèrous rival, then a mighty power
That makes its path at will, and every hour
Bears on its bosom fruit for good or ill,
Blesses the land—or curses by its will.—
And then the beauteous flowers that deck the
    field !
No human art can such pure rapture yield :
See, how they bloom in every opening dale !
See, how they kiss the soft, caressing gale !
Ah, how the heart is cheered if it but trace
These tinted smiles on Nature's lovely face !

  The pilgrim sought with calm and thoughtful
    mien
His homely cot, and left the glorious scene
For other eyes than his ; and softly sighed :
O beauteous earth ! O dark'ning human tide !

How joyous is the scene in all thy lands!
And all thy woes are born of human hands!
The time-worn wrecks along thy paths I trace
Bleach there thro' man's unkindness to his race.

THE SUCCESSION OF SPRING.

AURORA, from her lofty, burnished car,
  Sees Morning's torch glow with diminished flame;
    Bends to her steeds, points to the paling star,
    And links a warning with its goddess-name.
E'en as she speaks descends the needful change—
The quivering nostril answers gleaming eye:
They pant again ethereal depths to range,
And wake the echoes of the shadesome sky.
Up, up they wend from out the lambent east,
Driving huge, tossing clouds of tardy pace;
Now feel the slack'ning rein, and spring, released,
To toil the chariot through unmeasured space.

Aurora doth but heed, to bid them fly—
So eager she to please a fresh desire:
Yet pity dims the lustre of her eye
To burn again with an increasing fire.
For lo! she bears upon uplifted arms
A joyous infant whose celestial blush
Conveys the promise of expectant charms,
And shames the splendor of the morning flush.
Now stays the chase; she grasps a trembling wight;
Lampus and Phaeton wheel as with stretched hand
She plucks his garland, studded like the night,
And wills the infant brow support the band.
He, laughing, shakes his locks its frosts to fling.
Thus Winter was despoiled to crown the youthful Spring.

SONNET.

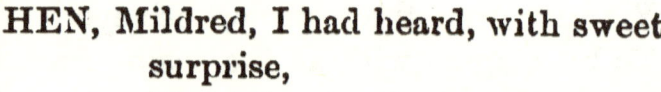HEN, Mildred, I had heard, with sweet surprise,
    An idle tale—in time bygone my own—
    Retold with pleasing harmony of tone,
    I could not, as I harken'd, but surmise:
Doth not there sleep within these depthless eyes
    A struggling fount whose waters, now unknown,
    Shall yet refresh—when 'tis maturer grown,
    When it reflects the ever-welcoming skies?
And, gazing on a fair, a faultless cheek
    Whose colors spoke the soul's untainted hue,
    In fancy watched arous'd emotions play
Ere yet obedient lips had learned to speak.
    An ardent wish upon the instant grew:
    Not distant be the dawning of that day!

ON THE SANDS.

WE looked on Ocean in her angriest
    mood :
The skies of sablest hue above her hung;
    The winds, at arms, aggressive, chill and
        rude,
    A loud defiance to her tossings flung ;
    And high above the stormy petrel sung
That note she loves when all around is gloom.
'Twas then, as forth that shrill storm-rhythm rung,
We saw beneath the deadly barrier loom
That lured yon laboring victim to a timeless doom.

Say, Ocean, which thy best beloved spoils ?
Are they alone the beautiful and fair
That breathe sweet life away within thy toils,
And tinge thy tonings with a deep despair ?
Should it not be alone thy constant care
To waft them to some certain happy end,
With smiles such as I oft have seen thee wear ?
Canst thou not cherished purposes defend
When they such costly aims shall to thy arms
    commend ?

We looked on Ocean—'twas her angriest phase—
Tumultuously surging at our feet.
In wonderment there learned her wondrous ways
Unheedful of the lowering mists that beat,
Unmarked as when the troubled main they meet.
Breathless, we note the towering billows bound
Till they the froward headland's front shall greet;
Feel the quick shock—the never ceasing sound
Breaks on the ear, and treads a never-ending round.

Say, Ocean, why should one, if formed to grace,
Trust to thy wiles? 'Tis to be torn and riven.
Is it with thine as with another race?
The promise fails that seemed most truly given:
The bark once gently fann'd now tempest driven.
She dreamed not as she lay where harbor locks,
Like some poor penitent that roams unshriven
Her calm presaged a storm of tireless shocks,—
For who can soothe the ire of the insatiate rocks?

We look'd, 'twas Ocean's most presumptuous hour:
When high she lifted up a threat'ning hand
And asked obedience to her gathering power
From the resisting, unsubmissive land.
She spread unshapely trophies on the strand

Whereon her seal unchangeable was set
That man might pause to of himself demand :
" What dwells there in this frame of mine that yet
Dares to contend with thee "—asks to himself forget.

Say, Ocean, why art thou enraged afresh ?
Yon monstrous surge ! if 't be thy might controls,
Turn it away from that within thy mesh
Ere a devouring tide upon it rolls !
Ah ! it must be as on life's treacherous shoals.
There, when ill-fated barks may not recede,
Destruction's ready mantle soon enfolds,
And prospering shapes, that scorned at thought of need,
Spread fragments far and near to blazon Ocean's greed.

We looked on Ocean in her angriest mood :
We could but linger—'t was a waking trance,
(We love her angriest and in solitude)
And, as we marked a giant form advance,
Knew the import of that last, eager glance
That deep into the soul its whisper tells :
'Tis here where angry Ocean toils and pants,
He rides supreme, and more 't would seem He dwells,
Than on the peaceful strand, on Ocean's troubled swells.

PSALM CXXVI.

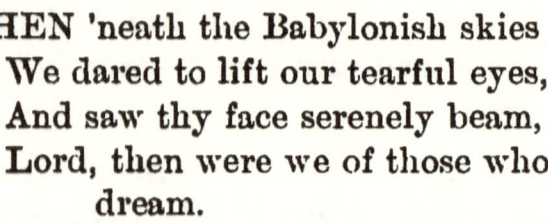
WHEN 'neath the Babylonish skies
We dared to lift our tearful eyes,
And saw thy face serenely beam,
Lord, then were we of those who dream.

Then were our mouths with laughter filled,
And joy our anxious bosoms thrilled;
The heathen cried in their dismay,
Why lead the captive host away?

Oh, wondrous! how Thy mighty deeds
More than suffice for mighty needs!
Though we were naked, faint, and sad,
Thy present care hath made us glad.

When in captivity we burned,
Thy hand the lash of bondage turned;
As banished Kedron southward flows,
So, Lord, again divert our woes.

That we may say, Though we in tears,
Have toiled a tedious span of years,
Our days, yet, Lord, shalt thou employ
To reap where we have sown in joy.

Let him that goeth forth to weep
A store of precious seedling keep :
He shall return with golden grain,
And joy abide with him again.

THE SUCCESSION OF SUMMER.

THROUGH the resplendent portal of the morn
    The rosy goddess guides her car again.
The shining steeds, subdued, of passion shorn,
    Press onward with the richly burdened wain.
Crouched at the goddess' feet, in flowery chains,
A lusty captive now her thought implores,
And waits the answer to his ardent strains.
Along the ruddy vault the chariot soars,
To stay anon within a fragrant bower.
Now, now her lips the ready answer frame :
"O youth, once joyous Spring, near is the hour—
The hour that parts thee from a potent name."
With the response, behold from out the night,
Of gracious aspect and of noble mien,
A presence come to charm his ravished sight
And pay an homage to the Morning Queen.

Aurora folds her in a close embrace,
And, turning from the suppliant's earnest gaze,
"For thee alone I may this crown displace.
Be thine the care of thrifty, fruitful days!"
Then o'er the prostrate boy she lingering bends
Ere from his locks the changeful crown she tears,
And to his gaze her laden hand extends;
Then to a beaming front the bauble bears:
The stripling veils his grief, accepts the vow—
Thus was young Spring despoiled to deck fair Summer's brow.

AT MOMENTS IN THE MONTH OF MANY ROSES.

AT moments, in the month of many roses,
    Than this my heart would every wish resign—
      To steal in silence where the one reposes
        Whose being cast a radiance over mine.

From absence can affection ne'er deliver,
  Or to the longing absent ones restore?

The answer is my heart's despairing quiver:
  "That radiance breaks upon thy life no
    more!"

Farewell! dear object of my adoration.
  Would that the grievous word could be unsaid!
That I might keep as mine this lonely station,
  And lay beside thine own a weary head!

WE WATCH THE DAWNING OF HER LIFE.

WE watch the dawning of her life
    Draw softly to a close;
  And all there is of thoughtless glee
    Give way to calm repose:
  We know as 'tis without portrayed,
    Within the seal is set,
  Though fair the dawning of her life,
    Her morn is fairer yet.

Glad was the dawning of the life
    Now merging into morn;
  Few were the clouds, and silver-tinged
    Upon its azure borne.

We cannot but foretell, as doth
    The watchman cry aloud,
"Fair dawn! fair morn! beyond the wave
    There hangs no shadowy cloud!"

And yet we would it were not so:
    The dawn hath sped so soon,
We fear the glory of her morn
    Will ripen into noon.
And then,—cease, cease, my anxious heart!
    Care may not spread his wings
Above the one whose echoed name
    Can sound thy secret strings.

We watch the dawning of her life
    Draw softly to a close—
So like the opening of the bud
    That gives the sweeter rose.
We say, "Fair dawn, that sent the hue
    Of promise that we see,
When thou art gone, and, too, the morn,
    How fair the noon will be!"

STRIKE, STRIKE THE HARP WITH LIGHTEST FINGER.

STRIKE, strike the harp with lightest finger;
  Again that mystic chord awake!
There's something, something that will linger
  After its waves of music break.

Minstrel, what happy moment brought thee
  Where music's votaries most dwell?
Minstrel, whose friendly hand hath taught thee
  To strike responsive chords so well?

Stay! did I not, enwrapt, bewondered,
  First hear that chord by Capri's shore?
And breathes it not of spirits sundered?
  Then, minstrel, wake that chord no more.

Yet on the midnight air 'twill tremble,
  Rising the mellow rays above.
Minstrel, that strain cannot dissemble—
  Thou strik'st the chord of hopeless love!

WHEN THOU ART GONE!

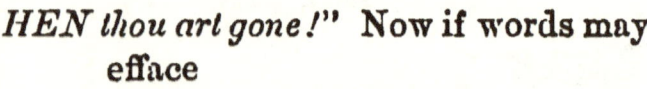"HEN *thou art gone!*" Now if words may efface
    Some passing thought outspoken by mischance,
  I pray thee speed them on in eager chase,
    Ere deeper in my heart than severing lance
Thy cry shall wound. Thy silence doth enhance
My gathering fears! Oh, canst thou not revoke
  What was so lightly uttered? Silence grants
No prosperous tale! When from my dreams I woke,
  There lay upon my heart the shadow of this stroke.

Guide of my infant steps, friend of my youth,
  I stop, appalled at thought of thee away.
Who now shall point me to the ways of truth,
  Or tell of error's taint and sure decay?
  So well I catch thy features' every play,
That ere thy lips an admonition framed,
  Mine eyes did seize it, that my steps obey.
Thou goest to the honored and the famed,—
  Yet fall, ye willing tears, and be no more ashamed!

"*Yet I could leave thee!*" 'Twas the cloud that lowered
  Over the brightest, swiftest hour that flew.
My spirit, too, would upward mount, empowered,
  And its quick course alone toward thee pursue.
  I would have had thee there ; and yet I knew
The self-same hours from thee went deeply fraught—
  Shadowed like mine. No more dismayed, and, too,
Armed with intent, I strove, renewed; and thought
How deeds impelled by love are well and swiftly wrought.

"*When thou art gone!*" Then struck the keenest dart
  That ever yet hath pierced a hidden goal.
Why shouldst thou go ? far better where thou art—
  Feeding the flame thou kindled'st in my soul.
  Let not thy tongue those distant scenes extol :
But rather stay it, till it me assure,—
  As doth yon timid dove that upward stole
To gaze upon the world. She, guileless, pure,
  Wheels to the cotter's roof, and knows herself secure.

WHEN I AM LOWLY LAID TO REST.

WHEN I am lowly laid to rest
    Oh, let it, let it be
Within the sound of curling crest;
And be the dirge I love the best
    Sung by the moaning sea.
And let it be so very near,
    My grave the sea beside,
That I may be—when they shall hear
How low I lie and they were dear—
    Bewept by every tide.

Oh, listen not if one shall say:
    Within this quiet vale
'Twere best he dream the hours away
Lulled by the brooklet's simple lay
    And sheltered from the gale.
Above the brooklet's voice should sound
    My never-ceasing sighs:
For never near its peaceful round
Could happy rest for me be found—
    Nor 'neath its silent skies.

Or if thy friend, with eye impearled,
   Point to the mountain bleak,
And say : His feet, when rudely whirled
The tempest, and its lightnings hurled,
   That spot were wont to seek.
Believe thou mayst ; but yet forfend
   To delve my humble bed :
I should not sleep though tempest rend
The ageless rock, and cypress bend
   Low o'er my restless head.

Oh, lay me here ! I'd only dwell
   With my beloved main !
Beneath the silver moon we tell
The secrets that we keep so well,
   To whisper o'er again :
And be it very, very near,
   This grave the sea beside,
That I may be—when they shall hear
How low I lie and they were dear—
   Bewept by every tide.

I WATCHED UPON A POINT OF BEATEN SAND.

 WATCHED upon a point of beaten sand,
    To see the silver moon grow softly bright:
I saw her rise—majestically and grand,
    To take her station as the Queen of Night.

Between that wave-worn shore and where she lay,
    Upon the peaceful ocean's distant rim,
There gleamed a band of many a fostered ray,
    Whilst all without was strangely weird and dim.

Upon the instant, starting from the black,
    There showed upon the bright a graceful thing:
She swept athwart the rippling, molten track,
    Then sought the darkness with her snowy wing.

"Ah, me!" I cry, "In my last fitful sleep,
    Thus did a beauteous vision come unseen,
Bathing an instant in a silvery deep,
    The next to hide as it had never been!"

LINES TO —–, AT LAKE GEORGE.

PON the glad to-morrow thou shalt
    wake,
  To wander in delight from vale to hill;
At eve in some light skiff thou'll skim
    yon lake
  And feel, perhaps, thy inmost spirit
    thrill—
Touched by its wondrous beauty. Now I see
  Thy dear, familiar face bend o'er the wave,
Wearing its mask of thoughtful revery;
  Now hear thee ask thyself: "Why was't God
    gave
This lake to lie unfathomed?" Then I'd say:
  "God hath his untold secrets; yet, I know
He did this in his goodness ('tis His way),
  That I to thee my depthless love might show.
This lakelet men have measured and have told,
  (And never depth will be men may not tell,)
But could thy dear, dark eyes my heart behold,
  Whence love's n'er failing springs of crystal well,
Thou'dst see love's lakelet there untold, un-
    fathomed dwell."

RUSSIAN HYMN.

(Histoire de Charles XII—Voltaire.)

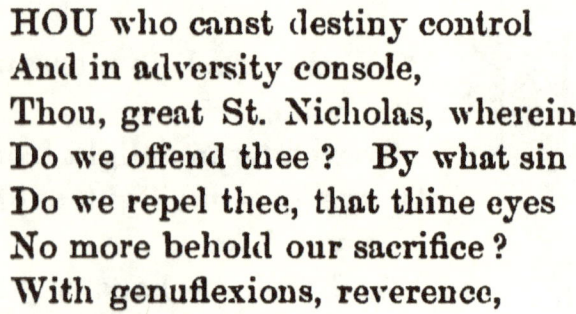THOU who canst destiny control
And in adversity console,
Thou, great St. Nicholas, wherein
Do we offend thee? By what sin
Do we repel thee, that thine eyes
No more behold our sacrifice?
With genuflexions, reverence,
We ask in vain for thy defense.
Though fervently we ever plead,
Thy face turns not upon our need.
If longer thou avert'st thine eye,
Unfortunates! we surely die!

See us, as sheep without the fold,
Our enemies grown fierce and bold,
Terrible, insolent, enraged,
Indomitable, unassuaged—
As lions robbed of young, and vex'd
With seeing us alone, perplexed.
They come that we may perish fast;
Their toils about our feet are cast;
And ere the saving veil of night,
Thousands shall vanish by their might:
If longer thou avert'st thine eye,
Unfortunates! we surely die.

St. Nicholas, thy saving hand—
Else we no longer may withstand.
Do thou again our standard bear,
And drive the foe within his lair;
Sorcerers are they and magic wield:
From power like this 'tis thou canst shield.
Mysterious spells long us enshroud:
Thy hand can brush away the cloud.
So we, distressed, thy people, call,
And look to see thee lift the pall:
If longer thou avert'st thine eye,
Unfortunates! we surely die.

THE MUEZZIN.

EARDST thou a cry from Byzas' turret walls
    Floating unsullied in the holy hush?
It is the muezzin's warning voice that falls
    On thine attentive ear. 'Tis while the rosy blush
Of the soft evening lingers. Hark! He calls
  The prayerful Moslem from the toil and rush
Of day's eventful scenes. He stops and kneels,
While to his heart the grateful missive steals.

Over swift flowing Bosphorus it flutters.
    See ! the barbarian holds his dripping oar.
He notes the cry the distant muezzin utters,
    And stays his hand to learn its meaning more.
His ear is all untaught ; he turns and mutters :
    Strangely 'twould sound from Tyras' wooded shore!
Then to his task with sturdier sinews bends,
As his rude prayer with the proud Moslem's blends.

The tawny sheik looks down from Uskudar—
    Amazement, awe and joy the scene begets ;
He thinks it naught that he has journeyed far,
    As he tells o'er a thousand minarets.
Hark ! Now above the sound of lute, guitar,
    Winning his thought from glittering spire and jet,
The muezzin's call dies on the evening air ;
His face turns to the skies—he clasps his hands in prayer.

The muezzin's holy call, it gilds the morn,
    Soothes at noon-tide and solaces at eve ;
It ebbs and flows by stately Golden Horn,
    And dies at last where Euxine's billows heave.
The felon sad, down sluggish Ister borne,
    Scorned of the prophet, when night's shadows weave,

Sinks in his clanking chains ; Hope's star is dim,
He knows the muezzin's voice speaks not to him.

Delight of Istamboul, thine eyes burn brightly,
   And richer glow thy cheeks than damask rose ;
Thy bosom bears its store of joy so lightly,
   Thou heed'st not Love, but triflest with his
      woes ;
Yet bends thy knee at morn, at noon and nightly—
   It is as forth Sophia's music flows ;
As through the ambient air, of liquid notes
The muezzin's wonted call to prayer floats.

Muezzin, men call thee blest. Oh, when alone
   In the deep night, or yet more lonely day,
Thou hark'nest to thy far-receding tone,
   And marvel'st that the sportive echoes play—
What then the many thoughts that are thine own ?
   'Tis not unhallowed pride thy cheeks betray !
As well thy voice in palaces may reign,
As o'er the homeless of the starlit plain.

THE SUCCESSION OF AUTUMN.

 AKE, sluggish Day! your eastern gate's
    ajar!
Aurora comes, O beauteous Queen of
    Morn!
    With measured pace the steeds propel
        her car,
    Oppressed with store of fruit and golden
        corn.
Within her gracious and encircling arm
Fair Summer gazes on the straining steeds
With pensive eyes, full of the nameless charm
That springs from thought of bounteous, goodly
    deeds.
    On toils the chariot to the dusky wood—
To stay at motion of uplifted hand.
Then speaks the goddess: All thou wrought'st is
    good,
Yet must I take again the magic wand.
Forth, Autumn, forth! Now 'tis for thee to reign!
Put on thy tinted robe, thy frosts distil,
Spread colors on the wide o'erteeming plain,
And with thy finger touch the verdured hill!

She speaks, and from the silent, dark'ning shade
A presence comes, in richest mantle clad,
Whose fitting homage to the queen is made,
With tears for Summer—desolate and sad.
Aurora must not heed—the wreath's unbound ;
On brow benignant now 'tis set. Behold
Who shares the burnished car--her beauty crowned
As morning rends the misty veil of gold ;
And who departs with troublous sigh restrained !
Thus Summer was despoiled and glorious Autumn
    reigned.

TO A SLEEPING CHILD.

SLEEPER, little sleeper mine,
  In this perfect sleep of thine.
Back to me, back to me,
  From the hills and sounding sea :
That thy dainty cheek and brown,
  Softer than the pillow's down,
Rests again so safely there,
  Heaven shall win a fervent prayer.

Folded, little, folded hands,
  Finished are the many plans ;

Tired, little, tired feet,
Summer wanderings are complete;
Lashes, laid o'er laughing eyes,
Seeing naught of butterflies—
That I see my treasure there,
Heaven may claim an ardent prayer.

Purling brooks and sunny beams,
I shall thank ye in my dreams:
'Tis her voice, 'tis her cheek
That your tender care bespeak;
Thine the praise for gems of health
Shining with her tresses' wealth.
Joy is mine: she sleepeth there!
Heaven shall win no sweeter prayer.

Sleeper, little sleeper mine,
In this guileless sleep of thine,
Low I bend, low I bend
Ere the words shall upward wend.
Back to me, back to me!
Drop the silken canopy.
That she's sleeping, sleeping there,—
Heaven ne'er won so fervent prayer.

EN GASCOGNE.

WHAT strange, contending passions war
    Within an erring mortal's breast!
Thoughts formed for utt'rance are withheld,
    For silence, are express'd.

'Twas yester eve: with mirth and wine
    We chased the happy hours along;
We chased the hours with mirth and wine,
    With laughter and with song.

It seems as if long days had passed,
    And yet it was but yester eve.
So lengthened are the little hours
    When we have cause to grieve.

And one was there with word and smile
    Whose beauty did each knight proclaim:
She stood by me and crowned the wine
    Beneath the astral-flame.

She knew I'd loved her long and well,
    (I've loved her from her tenderest years.)
And yet I'd never breathed of love—
    So fearful were my fears!

We were a brave, a revelling band,
    And I the gayest of the gay,
As in that Gascon hall we drank
    And chased the hours away.

I spoke, I know not why, some thought
    That grieved the lady when 'twas said:
I know because she ceased to smile
    And turned away her head.

She turned away her head; and then
    Turned back again with jest and smile,
And sought with even greater art
    The hours to beguile.

And though I louder laughed, and though
    I sang anew the boisterous song,
My eyes would seek the lady fair
    That I had seemed to wrong.

Could she forget? My chanson done
    She sang a measure of her own;
And laughed with voice as free from care
    And gleeful as my own.

I looked again, (yet smiles enwreathed
    The features of that lady dear,)
And saw it gathering on her cheek—
    The great and glistening tear.

I saw it swelling there, and then
  Upon her hand I saw it fall :
I flung afar my drinking-horn
  And fled that banquet-hall.

And 'tis for that I'm far away ;
  And 'tis for that I'd be alone ;
And 'tis for that I'm drifting now
  Adown the broad Garonne !

AUTUMN MUSINGS.

WHERE have I been, where have I been to-day ?
  Watching capricious billows at their play :
  They said : "The hours of man must troubled be !"
  And rolled along in restless ecstacy.

Where have I been to-day ? On yonder height,
Teaching an eaglet resting from his flight :
"Aspiring bird ! to rest, man doth despise !"
She spread her wings and mounted to the skies.

Where have I been to-day ? To feel, unseen,
The chill west wind that bloweth rude and keen.
It seemed to pause and mutter in its wrath:
"Thus blow I 'cross the wandering mortal's
    path."

Where have I been to-day ? I have been where
The forest trees are tossing cold and bare.
They wildly swayed their sturdy, leafless arms
And asked : "Doth man mourn his departed
    charms ?"

Where have I been to-day ? I have been down
Noting the falling leaf so crisp and brown.
It seemed to say—this broken, falling leaf—
"Doth man complain his mighty years are brief?"

Where have I been to-day ? Where prostrate lie
The fruits and flowers that in the autumn die.
I learn from them : "That as it is with man,
So blossom they and perish in a span."

I have been forth to Nature brown and sere—
Befitting garment for the dying year :
The year will surely die ;—O bliss to me—
My steadfast hope for immortality !

* * * * *

I would not, and I need not, think
    That He who me my being gave,
Will quench it at th' appalling brink
    That walls about the shadowy grave.

Nay, nay ; not so : each sense rebels;
    The tongue rejects the painful words :
My spirit that each planet tells !
    That courses like the flight of birds !

It seems endued for endless time :
    Eternity were not too much.
My spirit as the changeful clime !
    Oblivion in an autumn-touch !

Yon cloudlet on the mountain's brow
    And I, must ours be kindred fates ?
It hangs a moment there—and now
    In air forever dissipates.

No ; longer than the burning sun
    Will live the better part of me :
He wastes, his measured journey done :
    I am for all eternity.

THE SUCCESSION OF WINTER.

AND now the vap'rous East begins to glow—
   A token that the Morning Queen is near;
   Now widening tints of pearl and sapphire show;
   Now beams of splendor guide the charioteer.
Why slowly rides the queen? why bows her head
As if for grieving piteous cause she had?
Aurora mourns for Autumn, who is dead,
And fitly comes in sombre garments clad.
The trembling steeds, with cautious step and slow,
And backward turning of reluctant eyes,
Propel the burnished car through frost and snow,
And much lament warm Orient's softer skies.
"Speed, Lampus, speed! nor thou, good Phæton, yield!"
It is the sorrowing goddess gently calls,
"Upon the tablet of the whitening field
I would proclaim the solemn funerals!"
Who can the rosy goddess' will withstand?
Her chariot rests amid the frozen plains:
One hand her face doth veil; her sceptre-hand

Lifts Autumn's crown.   Soft! decked in glittering
    chains,
A spectre comes with crafty, silent pace:
He steals upon the goddess unbeknown,
She heedeth not, so lowly droops her face,
He grasps the crown; he wears it for his own;
With mocking laugh the naked wood regains.
Thus Autumn was despoiled—and ruthless Winter
    reigns.

"VENUS IS AGAIN THE EVENING STAR."

  THOU fairest orb of all the night,
   We welcome thine effulgent ray,
  That holds in chains the waning light,
   And bids night's shades away.
  With softest flame, sweet Venus, rise
  To reign the queen of western skies!

For thee we've sighed, when to adorn
  The eastern skies thou wast installed,
And with thy splendor lit the morn,
  And shone on eyes enthralled;
Forerunner of the king of day
Whose fiery flood usurped thy sway.

Now dost thou follow in his train,
  Tho' but to linger one brief hour.
What rival shall thy beauty wane
  Or spoil thee of thy dower?
With rapturous joy by mortals seen
Thou floatest there, pure, radiant queen!

Venus, thou loveliest Evening Star!
  How can we ever say farewell?
Never forgotten, tho' afar!
  Long we for thy magic spell.
Fair lamp of eve, there calmly rest;
Shed joy and peace to every breast!

THE LANGUAGE OF THE SEA.

SINGING, singing one refrain!—
  Tell me, ever changing sea,
What so oft I've asked in vain—
  Break the secret now to me.
Flowing, flowing to the shore,
  From some lonely far off clime,
Here thine ebbing life to pour
In unceasing, saddening rhyme.
Sighing, sighing ever so!—
Do the memories fill thy breast

Of some deep lagoon where flow
Emerald floods o'er coral crest?
Swelling with the monsoon's wrath,
Of some vast and sparkling ocean,
On thy solitary path
Wafted with unheeded motion.
Tell me, too, of pitiless storms,
When, beneath the blackening skies
Lift thy waves in giant forms
As resistless whirlwinds rise.
Sweeping o'er many a nameless grave—
Trophies to thy power and might;
O'er the fairest and the brave,
Who embraced thee with affright.
O, thou deep, mysterious sea!
Coming now, and now receding—
Secret none I'll win from thee,
Whisper none save thy sad pleading!

THE EVENING WALK.

WHEN twilight's softest breezes gently rise,
  Bearing upon their course the clouds of fire,
And rarest, golden tints stain o'er the skies,
  What peaceful, pensive moods the heart inspire!

When twilight's shades anon come softly stealing,
  How soothing then, alone, to walk abroad,
While Nature sleeps, her every charm revealing,
  Soon wins the weary heart to true accord.

When twilight's dark'ning pall at length descending,
  Displays the glittering treasures of the night,
Of orbs and constellations never ending,
  How bows the heart before His power and might!

May that long twilight, ever nearing, nearing,
  Glow with rich hues of hopes divinely fair!
May that last, dark, mysterious pall, when clearing,
  Show Thy bright, guiding presence waiting there!

TO THE ROBIN IN APRIL.

O SWEET robin redbreast!
    Thy blithesome note I hear,
A welcome, welcome sound
    Delights my listening ear;
And tells of dreary winter past,
And blooming spring-time come at
        last.

O sweet robin redbreast!
    Each morning let thy voice
Pour forth its hymn of praise,
    And with my own rejoice.
The Prince of Spring-time young and fair,
Hath strewn his treasures everywhere!

O sweet robin redbreast!
    Let not the icy air
Subdue thy swelling song,
    Nor lead thee to despair;
With rich profusion, leaf and flower
Will soon perfume thy hidden bower.

O sweet robin redbreast,
   How sweet thy ringing strain!
It seems to tell of clouds dispelled
   And sunshine come again:
It seems to say, with tuneful art,
The dawn is near; up, drooping heart!

THE INVITATION.

(Suggested by Corinna going a-maying.)

COME, up, my love!
   And quickly don
   Thy field attire;
   For, grandly on
   That steed of fire,
   The sun, ascends
     above.
For shame! sweet sluggard, banish hurtful sleep,
And drink of Nature's nectar long and deep!

   Stay not, but up!
     These gems of dew,
   Like diamonds rare,
     Are known to few;

Yet, jewel ne'er so fair
   E're shone in crown or cup.
On morning glory's bell securely clinging,
Wherever violet banks are coyly springing!

  Haste! love, across
    Thro' field and fold,
  In dark, wild wood,
    With spots of gold;
  As conquerors should,
    We'll rest on throne of moss.
For thee a crown I should be weaving now,—
The fairest ever pressed thy golden brow!

  Then haste, my love!
    Too quickly fly
  Life's rosy hours;
    Too quickly die
  Dew drops and flowers;
    Too soon the steed's above.
Then haste, O, haste, dear love, we'll seize each
    prize
Of May-morn, field, and happy, blushing skies!

DOWN WHERE THE SEA AND RIVERS MEET.

KNOW a secret shore—and low;
  Sequestered and well loved retreat!
'Tis there the rippling wavelets flow,—
  Down where the sea and rivers meet.

You'd say a spot so drear—apart,
  So wild, companionless—alone,
Possessed no sweet, seductive art,
  No gentle language of its own.

Oh, yes! and often I have brought,
  From hurrying throngs, oppressing cares,
And told them there; and there been taught
  Content e'en fitful ocean shares.

The ocean! unalloyed delight
  To note each varying phase and change
Its face portrays, of shade or light,
  As zephyrs sweep or cloudlets range.

I love it for the friends I've made—
    The laughing wave, and dark browed rock
In dripping robes of moss arrayed,
    Secure from ocean's every shock.

There, too, the seagull's piping notes
    Give to the waves a plaintive strain,
As homeless on the gale she floats,
    Or bosoms on the treacherous main.

Far distant be the unwelcome lot
    That bars from thence my hastening feet!
And may their imprints vanish not,—
    Down where the sea and rivers meet.

TO MY SISTER.

AH! sister sweet, e'er long to greet
   An absent one with fondest word;
Thine own kind smile will soon beguile
   A heart with joyous visions stirred.

By love made bright, in quick delight
   Thine eyes will beam for me once more;
E'en as some ray, sped on its way,
   Proclaims the wanderer's voyage o'er.

What welcome cheer thy voice to hear,
   When come again those pleasant hours
In whispering glade, in dark'ning shade,
   'Mid waving fields and blossoming flowers!

With daintiest care, in colors rare,
   Proud nature may her robe adorn;
Be thou but there, to me more fair
   Art thou than countless gems of morn.

And when at eve soft zephyrs breathe,
   And golden flames die in the west,—
E'en that calm hour hath not the power
   That lives within thy gentle breast.

ANTONY'S LAMENT OVER CÆSAR.
[*Julius Cæsar.*]

TH' appalling deed is done!
 A mighty form forever prostrate lies,
 And quenched fore'er the lightnings in those eyes;
  The tyrant's arm has won;
And Cæsar from a hundred wounds doth bleed,
A hundred tongueless mouths in anguish plead.

 There bows his only friend!
Within his arms he folds that matchless head,
And on its brow his burning tears are shed;
  While yet attend
The mad, tumultuous throng, and curses ring
Above the clay they almost hailed a king.

 And thou, laid low!
To other conquests, then, thy spirit hastes,
And leaves to me this crimson flood that wastes.
  Thou wil'st it so!
And yet not so; thy spirit fled, to soar
To fresher conquests on that unknown shore.

Oh, ruthless fate !
Immortal Cæsar ! whilst thy princely blood
Thus pours along, beside that unknown flood
      Thy soul doth wait
To see thine Antony his love-vows keep,
And all thy foes to foul destruction sweep.

      Then, spirit, rest !
Thy dear loved friend to thee is not untrue,
And unborn millions yet shall call one true—
      Him, Antony ; and best
Of all that noble band once in thy train,
Who held their loves as thine—poor loves, how
  vain !

      For Cæsar's love,
Ye howling wolves, behold this piteous sight !
This lyre unstrung—this sun robb'd of its light.
      Nor high above,
His mighty arm, Olympian Jove's proud lance,
At Conquest's voice shall ever more advance.

      There low he lies !
Ye worse than slaves, or hideous creeping thing,
Look on his weeping wounds. So, tears will spring
      To your stern eyes !
Oh, let them forth—nor longer stay them there !
Such precious drops should temper my despair.

And I may speak?
Then let great Cæsar's virtues be my theme—
That endless chain of deeds, that, like a dream
    Of winter's night, would seek
To paint its vivid pictures on the brain,
And then in envy paint them o'er again.

    Was he not great
While yet in untried youth, by stern decree,
Dread Scylla wills: "Cornelia's love for me"?
    He spurns his high estate;
And for her love the tyrant's land is flown,
And chastely Cæsar waits for her alone.

    See with what store
From all the great and wise he decks his mind,
The fruit of which he showers on his kind;
    How he implores
Of Rome's propitious gods that hour to greet
That sees the world sit smiling at her feet.

    Undaunted, calm,
He sweeps unconquered ever; at his name
Exhaustless spoil and lands grace proud Rome's
    fame.
    Hers is the palm:
The East, Spain, Gaul, and Britain, each the prize
To this resplendent bolt Tarpeius flies.

   For Rome and you,
Once happy Romans! Can your list'ning ears
Be dulled so soon? Flow on, ye pitying tears,
   And prove, if true,
The love ye bore; and, sorrowing torrents, meet
To wash these stains from wondering Pompey's
  feet!

   Could but a glow
This brazen statue's eyes now animate,
Think ye that they would triumph o'er the state
   Of their great foe?
The noble Pompey's eyes would scorn the deed,
And his great heart for this poor hart would
  bleed.

   Look on his brow
Where, at your bidding, I the laurel placed;
See how his soul its beauty there has traced!
   Where roams it now?
Soft! let me in his crimson raiment fold
The god-like face we may no more behold.

   Here let them rest—
The mighty arms a thousand tribes that smote,
The skillful hands, his deathless records wrote,—
   Stilled with his breast!
The impious thieves have dared to force and rob;
The noble Cæsar's soul has ceased to throb.

Aye, now ye weep!
Tumultuous passions wrap your souls in fire!
Let Furies will these traitors in their ire
      Tantalus' sleepless sleep!
While all true Romans shudder as they tell
How liberty, by Brutus' dagger, fell!

ALONE.

'VE wandered by the whispering sea,
  For it the world beside forsaking;
Its joyous echoes spoke to me—
  They were not wild waves idly breaking.
    And yet,
Tho' oft I've heard them call before,
The voice was not the voice of yore.

I've stood upon the golden crest,
  And watched the twilight's gathering shade;
The summer sun sank to his rest,
  Where all his glimmering glories fade.

'Tis strange—
Tho' oft I've seen his rays before,
The light was not the light of yore.

Dear Heart! 'tis since thou art not by.
  The sea's glad echoing voice was thine;
The glories of that western sky,
  Thy bright eyes wingéd back to mine.
    Ah, yes!
It was thy presence near me there
That made the summer scene so fair.

THE LOST TREASURE.

WITHIN a hall of royal state
  With richest canopies o'erspread-
      ing,
  Where sculptured shapes in ambush
      wait,
    A flickering lamp its beams is
      shedding;
But scarce its quivering ray reveals
The form that thro' the stillness steals.

The sovereign of a thousand lords,—
    A monarch, whose soft-breathed command
Would gather to his glittering boards
    The brave and loveliest of the land,—
Bows there in contemplative mood,
Akin to the deep solitude.

    Hour upon hour has slowly pressed,
        When from his posture of despair
    He rises now, and from his breast
        He frees the hands long claspéd there;
And from his brow he lifts the band,
And tears the signet from his hand.

    Then through the court the signal speeds,
        Calling wise counsellors to attend,
    To reap the fruit that wisdom breeds,
        That age and ripe experience lend.
Now to the summons' echoing sound
The fathers quickly gather round.

    "Wait we, great master, thy command,"
        Sulpucianus 'twas that spake,
    "Name but thy wish by sea or land,
        'Soever course our ensigns take—
Be it cold Caledonia's heath,
Or realms of burning sands beneath;

"From fair Campania's vine-clad plain;
    Along the broad Flaminian Way,
Where wide-spread Orient's soft domain
    Welcomes thine undisputed sway.
Hast not the thing thou wouldst possess,
Breathe but its name—the wish express."

The monarch hears with mien benign,
    Views long the vassals at his feet,
Leaves his high state with gracious sign,
    And kindly words their fealty greet.
"O fathers! not what I would taste,
But mine I fain would have replaced.

"For as the sun old Tiber sank beneath,
    A prize had flown, dearer than captive train,
Or sparkling jewel princes may bequeath:
    A day has passed, and I have lived in vain—
No trophy from the field of knowledge won,
No thought engrossed, no virtuous action done."

WOULD DAY WERE COME!

WOULD day were come! ah, me! I cannot bear
   To welcome now the silvery moonlight beams;
Nor listen to the strains that fill the air,—
   Like some unfeeling mirth to me it seems.

And ye, bright stars, hide your reproachful light
   That fain would win me from my darling's glance.
Do ye not know her eyes are dimmed to-night—
   Her laughing eyes, that oft my heart entrance?

Ye fragrant winds, so gently stealing by,
   I think ye know my darling's voice is stilled;
That her sweet song has vanished in a sigh—
   Her ringing voice that oft my bosom thrilled.

Until her eyes shall light again with glee,
   And silvery sweet the music of her voice
In wavering notes comes o'er the air to me,
   No charm have ye that can my heart rejoice.

Would day were come to speed night's shades
    away !
  What cheer bring ye, ah, me, ye wearying
    hours ?
She loved the day, the bright and glorious day,
  Its sunny warmth, its singing birds and flowers.

DEUS MEUS ! DEUS MEUS !

(Inscription on a memorial church bell.)

EBBING, swelling,
  Falls there not upon thine ear,
    Whispering, telling,
  In an accent deep and clear ;
    And ever thus—
Deus Meus ! Deus Meus !

    Sweetly ringing
In dewy glades, at early morn ;
    Its passion bringing
Into my thought, and lightly borne ;
    And ever thus—
Deus Meus ! Deus Meus !

Booming, clanging
O'er hastening crowds—in maddening strife;
Lowering, hanging,
A pendant blade, that parts some life;
And ever thus—
Deus Meus! Deus Meus!

Wavering, stealing
Where pleasure reigns, where beauty glances;
Softly appealing
To some breast that love entrances;
And ever thus—
Deus Meus! Deus Meus!

Clustering, thronging
To Meditation's thoughtful hour;
Waiting, longing
For some behest beyond her power;
And ever thus—
Deus Meus! Deus Meus!

Whispering, sighing
Some cadence while the spirit sleeps;
Sinking, dying,
As Care, forgotten, waits and weeps;
And ever thus—
Deus Meus! Deus Meus!

THE REVELLERS.

WHEN this old world was young,
    (A weary, weary while away)
'Tis said, mid vales and woods among,
    The bright-eyed fairy folk did play;—
That from their tiny, secret bowers,
    When shone the earliest moonlight beam,
They came to dance away the hours,
    And pleasure reigned supreme.

'Tis said such pastimes ne'er were seen ;
    For, as they formed and madly danced,
From every flower on mead and green
    On which the silvery moonlight glanced,
Some kinsman of each little sprite
    Would break the portals of his cell,
And join the revels of delight,—
    So 'witching was the spell.

Thus passed the hours of dear delight
    Till softest Zephyr's whispering sigh
Bade each sweet fairy say good night,—
    For blushes tinge the sky ;
Then round their queen, clasped hand to hand,
    They still the music of their bells

And fade, when sinks her dewy wand,
  To their own woods and dells.

But these revellers far have fled,
  (The world's so very wise and cold)
And tho' the same soft beams are shed
  No flowery portal will unfold.
Perhaps from yon bright distant star,
  Or from some secret, deepest glade,
The night winds bear the tale afar
  Of fairy revellings play'd.

TO A FRIEND.

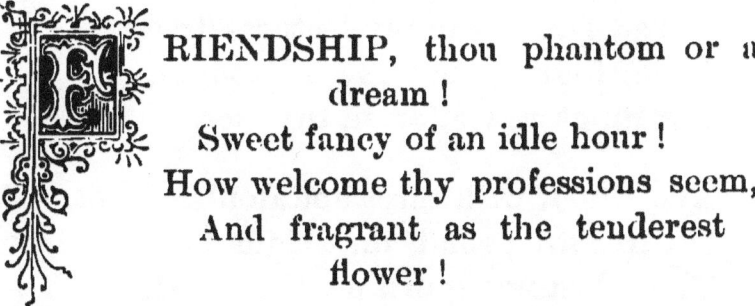

FRIENDSHIP, thou phantom or a
    dream!
  Sweet fancy of an idle hour!
How welcome thy professions seem,
  And fragrant as the tenderest
    flower!

Friendship, thou bubble rich in hue,
  That on the summer air is borne!
Is thy bright substance ever true?
  Wouldst glow of thy pretences shorn?

Friendship, thou calm, unruffled lake!
  'Twould seem that thou must ever sleep:
Yet, should the gentlest zephyr wake,
  Wouldst thou that fleeting promise keep?

With such poor, undeserving arts
  Do transient friendship's show beguile;
A glow the summer day imparts,
  But shuns the adverse wintry trial.

Then how complacently I view
  Thy friendship, firm, unshaken, sure,—
Since passing years have told how true
  And changeless it can be—and pure.

Should calm contentments guide my thought,
  And symbols in my features trace,
I ever found, when there I sought,
  A quick reflection in thy face.

And when, with cares and doubts beset,
  I free my proud, imperious will,
Thou dost not spurn me then, but, yet,
  Thou shed'st a tear—and lov'st me still.

MY ARGOSIES.

MY beautiful fleet has sailed away,—
  I watched them, standing on the sand,—
My white-winged fleet will come home some day,
  Bringing me treasures from every land;
For I've made them promise—the winds and the gales—
That they'll lovingly watch o'er my fleet that sails.

Over the tumbling and stormy deep,
  My well-manned fleet will laugh to scorn
(Well-manned, if wishes can vigils keep)
  The warning wrecks that, beaten and torn,
Drift ever and ever, but warning in vain.
My fleet shall come sailing home over the main.

My sturdiest ship hath ribs of oak
  And deep full lines, to buffet the shore.
What cares she for the whirlwind's stroke?
  Smiling she'll welcome old ocean's roar.
Sometimes, I fear me, she floats too deep
To bring me the treasures I fain would reap.

I sometimes fear for my fairest bark,
    That I've fashioned the happiest sea to sail;
To gain it the ocean's so wide and dark,
    Her sails are of silk and her masts are so frail.—
My heart seems to tell me, from yon golden shore,
My bark will ne'er come to add wealth to my store.

In my fleet are many of graceful form,—
    I am sure they will swiftly skim the seas,—
But then will they watch for the pitiless storm?
    Ah, me! they are trimmed for the balmiest breeze;
I fear that my fair-weather sailors will sleep:—
Then my sailors and treasures ne'er will come from the deep.

Some day thro' the golden, summer sea
    (Till then, how oft shall I seek this shore?)
My white-winged fleet will be wafted to me,
    With its priceless treasures. I'll tell them o'er;
Then should fortune, sweet love, idle joys, soothe my breast,
In some calm, peaceful port may my Argosies rest.

THE WAGER.

[Their debts of honor were discharged with the utmost fidelity. The desperate gamester, who had staked his person and liberty on the last throw of the dice, submitted to the decision of fortune, and suffered himself to be bound and sold into remote slavery by his weaker but more successful antagonist.]

SUEVIAN, bring the shameful chain
   For my hands—my heart has fled!
Bind this too strong arm again—
   Its pulseless current is not dead:
The flame my bold sire's deeds intrenched,
   Within this bosom brightly burns.
Would my dark destiny had quenched
   The fate my spirit spurns!

Comrade! I thought to win thy gold;
   But, comrade, all I have is thine;
And more besides, a thousand fold—
   For gold I waged myself divine.
For idle hours I sought it not,—
   The mountain doth reward my toil,—
I thought to bless a fair one's lot,
   And deck her with thy spoil.

Northman ! take this eaglet's plume.
    Thou shalt lead my chosen band,
Exalted chief. Helvetia's doom—
    To languish in a stranger's land.
Yet from thee one last boon I crave,—
    Then easier shall my bondage seem,—
In the fierce onset let it wave—
    There let its pinions stream !

Warrior ! when from our forest-north,
    At signal from that fluttering crest,
Her fair, unnumbered sons steal forth
    O'er Danube's spotless, frozen breast,—
I'll listen to her muttering sound,
    While dazzling sunbeams glance :
Then a proud freeman's soul shall bound—
    I'll claim my plume and lance !

THE FORTUNATE ISLES OF THE BLESS'D.

SAY, where are the far and the famed
    blessèd isles,
  Where the voice of the murmuring water
    beguiles,
    And the voyager's ever at rest;
  Where music's the song of the guardian
    seas,
Gently borne on the tale-bearing wings of the
    breeze—
  O! where are the Isles of the Bless'd?

Just beyond, where uplifted the great pillars
    tower,
Ever loiters Atlanticus' vigilant power,
    Lurking low in remorseless quest;
If I knew not his name, and how fatal his wiles,
Enticed by his azurine hue and his smiles,
    I should seek for the Isles of the Bless'd.

Perchance, 'neath yon dreaded and frown-bearing
    height,
Undaunted, some bark takes her perilous flight,
    By the winds and the waters caress'd.
O! happy, that intrepid, unbaffled prow!

O! happy, that bold, way-worn mariner now
  Swiftly nearing the Isles of the Bless'd!

Entrancing the scenes that his quick senses fill,
As unchecked, unrestrained, deep in vale, over hill,
  His swift, flying footsteps are press'd.
Could a scene ever fairer than this prospect rise—
The sounds, the dark verdure, the fragrant-swept skies,
  Of these fam'd blessed Isles of the Bless'd?

Shall Conflict's dire din, be it never so rude,
These lone, peaceful latitudes dare to intrude,
  To jar on his now fancied rest?
Shall cold Envy chill the friend once held so near,
Or grim Slander's pale apparition appear
  In these far away Isles of the Bless'd?

O! haste, blesséd Islander! surely wing back
Some token to guide thro' thine own furrowed track,
  Be it ever the East or the West;
That I, undismayed, truly searching my chart,
May find, O sweet bliss! in its happiest part,
  The fortunate Isles of the Bless'd!

MOTHERLESS.

ONE eve, in fancy's idle mood,
My listless way alone pursued,
    A cry came low and clear.
It was, methought, the saddest sound
That ever yet its way had found
    To an unwilling ear.

Ere that, and often, I had read
Of cruel wars, and havoc spread,
    And varied tales of woe;
But turmoils, flaming fields, and slain,
Brought to my bosom no such pain,
    Nor dimmed my vision so.

Transfixed, I listened, if again
That note should flutter—but in vain,
    I only heard my heart:
I looked, and lo! a stately pile
To cheer dark, orphaned childhood's trial
    Essays the parent's part.

And yet, secure within that fold,
Unreconciled, and uncontrolled,
    Thus plead affection's wants:

E'en there, with every need supplied,
Some vision, absent from its side,
    The tender memory haunts.

I turned, and softly breathed a prayer—
That none endeared to me should share
    Those hospitable walls :
That no tear-stainéd, artless cheek
Should there its orphaned pillow seek,
    As deeply darkness palls.

DEATH OF JULIAN CHLORUS.

COMRADES, bend low, the certain hour draws near :
But, hasten to soever fate befalls,
Death's summons unconcernedlyI hear—
A willing subject the destroyer calls.
And, since humanity cannot delay
    The still, resistless voice that bids him shape,
And since proud monarch cannot disobey
    The hand that points the way he would escape,—

Man's common lot is his—he surely dies
  And leaves behind a pale, unsightly frame
At length to moulder, whilst the spirit hies
  To airy scenes remote—a living flame.
Then should I, knowing, rather not rejoice
  With cheerfulness, content, and ready will;
And give my speedy answer to the voice
  Most trustingly, and bid again be still
The tongue that fain would tempt an unsought
    stay?
  Let mine be wisdom's part, purer and better.
A cheerful acquiescence spurns delay,
  And well befits the honest, ready debtor.
So, this unstable body frees its soul—
  Onward it speeds, and ever joyously
With other thronging myriads, to the goal;
  And, once admitted there, forever free
From lingering, irksome doubts. How poor and
    vain
  The fragile casement we inhabit here
To that celestial, gleaming form we gain:
  How gross its once prized attributes appear!
Should brooding, deep regrets for this estate
  The weary evening-hour of age employ?
Nay, rather is it pleased to separate
  From ceaseless labor for the realms of joy.
The dearest, fondest transports that await

  The soul of purest, provéd piety,
Are unapproached, save through the single gate
  That shuts without the world's anxiety.
Be not this welcome, coming stroke bewept,
  Since honors, even to satiety,
The gracious gods have brought me to accept
  With fair renown. Ambition's cup is filled
With unthought richness. History's page,
  Unsullied, bears no blood-stained trace
Of cruel deeds ; no tyrant's withering rage
  Taints o'er my name to live, and I displaced.
So, since my journey ended free from guile,
  Welcome the word ! Contented with my loss,
Undaunted, death I view, and with a smile.
  Untarnished and yet free from dark remorse,
Conscious I am how purely hath been kept
  The trust committed by the divine power ;
How, waking, 'twas my thought ; and, when I slept,
  It was the vision of the deep, night-hour ;
And undissembling, often have I wept,
  Lest undefiled I should not yield my dower.
Then, how serenely may I not reflect
  Upon the crown that waits beyond the tide !
And what fair portion may I not expect,
  When in its peaceful ways my steps abide !—
Ever detesting, in this restless sphere,
  The despot's maxims, whose fair words may hide

Oppression's horrid hand, that quick uprears
    To crush so'er unjust suspicion spied,
And knows no spot uncurst by idle fears,
    And falls a victim to his own vain pride.
My every act to prudence gave quick ear,
    Or from experience craved a guiding word;
Justice, my jewel, knew nor threat nor tear;
    Honor but due, the chaplet saw conferred.
How have I labored in the cause of peace,
    If, haply, Peace brought in her smiling train
The people's weal, and Nature's glad increase;
    That chief reward,—since Ceres sought in vain
All art aids not, and wanton luxuries cease.
    But, did the rude barbarian lift to smite—
A long farewell to her endearing charms,
    Till he his dark recesses sought in flight,
There to bewail the soldier's ponderous arms,
    Invincible and boundless in their might
E'en tho' the Fates had whispered their alarms,
    And I had learned by divination's art
That I must fall from battle's hurtful harms,
    And with immortal heroes claim my part.
O this hath been my soul's oft-told desire!
    For now no traitor's steel within this heart
Bids it be still,—no lingering ills aspire
    By slow, insidious measures, dealt unseen,
This tenement to bathe in quenchless fire,

And blast to sterile boughs the oak once green;
But, like a fortressed and sustainéd tower,
　　That hath withstood beleaguering, warlike foes,
Reel to the dust before some honored power,
　　And in my ruin bury all my woes.

ASLEEP.

PAUSED where Innocency slept,—
　　It was the deep and silent night,—
I lingered, as the moments swept.
Sweet watch I with the angel kept.
　　Fair picture! Page of pure delight!

We smiled, because our darling smiled.
　　Some joyous pastime of the day,
By which her rosy hours are whiled,
E'en 'cross that stream her heart beguiled,
　　O'er memory held its tender sway.

We sighed, because our darling sighed.
　　Some childhood's care within her breast,

Unbidden, dared to float the tide
And bear its shadow to her side,
   To mar that calm and perfect rest.

And, nightly, at that sacred place
   My heart's o'erflowing raptures pour:
No burning lines that poets trace
For me have charms, when that fair face
   Portrays its sweet and varying lore.

HOLLYWOOD.

(Hollywood Cemetery, Richmond, Virginia, where lie buried five thousand Confederate dead.)

FAIR Hollywood, within thy peaceful shade
   A stranger comes, and muses o'er the scene.
Thou heed'st not tho' a wanderer's feet have strayed,
   Lured by thy robe of autumn's variant sheen.

Fair Hollywood, of those who lowly sleep,
   There is not one who softly called him friend;

The accents of his name, no tongue may keep,
    Of all who to their rest thy paths shall wend.

Fair Hollywood, the countless, unmarked mounds
    That, undulating, cloy thy widening vale,
Impen forever in their chilling bounds
    The wearied part that steps not o'er Death's pale.

Fair Hollywood, dread memories of that past,
    That gave these treasures to thy cold embrace,
No dark aspersions on their fate shall cast,
    Nor bring an untoward presence near thy place.

Fair Hollywood, thy crimson, deeply hued,
    Tells of no strife diffusing o'er the plain;
Thy waving arms speak of no steel imbued.
    Contending passions sleep in thy domain.

Fair Hollywood, the stranger's eyes now turn
    To low, sequestered spots where rest the dead,
In massive tomb with ostentatious urn
    And glowing transcripts of their tenants spread.

Fair Hollywood, when in his distant home
    Pure recollections of thy features rise,
'Tis not of these he'll write in memory's tome,
    Not of thy grandeur, nor the great and wise.

No ; 'tis that vine-decked pile the sky aspires—
  A fostered trophy memory bears from thee ;
Mid those who sank beneath the withering fires,
  Memoria in æterna shall it be.

THE SACRILEGE OF ALARIC.

COULD Melpomene my tongue inspire !
O for Apollo's all-responsive lyre !
Then should my soul no slothful utter-
    ance brook,
  And deathless write my words in Clio's
    book ;
  Then should I dare to climb the sacred
    mount
And drink with her the sweet Castalian fount.
Gifted by these, from Hellas' every vale,
A voice should spring to cry afar the tale
Of her dread death ; from the Saronic bay,
Where young Hyperion greets the earliest day,
To the far point that tells the Arcarnian plain
Where sinks his steed to spring refreshed again ;

From snow-crowned Ossa, where the gods abide—
Fair realm of Tempe, Peneus flood beside—
Borne on the soft, Argolian zephyr's wings,
E'en to the foam whence dark Cythera springs,
Should rise the dirge, and, in its plaintive moan
Tell of this land—its glories—glories flown.

Could the heroic Theseus in his dreams,
Have known that ever Phœbus' darting beams
Should show this sight; his oft stained sword that foiled
The Marathonian herd, whose rage despoiled
Athena's state—had never idly slept,
But on Parnassus' brow its vigils kept.

Had divine Pallas,—she whose skillful hand
Brought peace and beauty to her mighty land,
When forth from Zeus' brow, with war-like mien,
All armed she sprang,—had Pallas then but seen
The thread that Clotho's ever-turning reel
Spun for her love, her hand had stayed the wheel.
No spirit wandering those fair fields along
Shall by its will or wishes fly the throng,
Nor bend to Lethe's torrent, and lift up
The mystic draught that sleeps within the cup:
For what purged soul would crave a sight like this,

Or here, renewed, forget Elysium's bliss ?

* * * * * *

Behold Alaric, scourge and dread of kings,
With high disdain turns from the war-worn wastes;
   Upon th' impatient steed in armor springs,
And leads the way his ruthless hand has traced.
   See at his back the wild Borysth'ian horde,
Strong in their pride and eager for the fray,
   Forth from each fastness, as a deluge poured,
O'er all the peopled vales that stretch away—
   From high Olympus, capped with glistening
      snows,
From Achaian marts and Elis' sacred plains,
   Beyond where Corinth's sparkling water flows
And o'er its bosom waft Arcadian strains.
   On come the hosts ! no power to impede :
Their eager steps approach the Malian bay,
   Like foul Chimæra in hot rage and speed,
While Bellerophon sleeps, no hand to stay
   The march victorious : mount the glorious rock
Where the brave hundreds, every breast a tower,
   Kept well the pass, nor yielded to the shock
Of Persian cohort till death quelled their power.
   O sprang no virtue from so bold a sire
To kindle spark of ardor in the son ?
   Alas ! there glows within no valorous fire !

The god-like race had died ere but begun ;
    And in their craven breasts the patriot flame
Is of a pale and feeble, unreal hue :—
    Sparta lives not, and honor's but a name.

Now doth the deluge stifle in its rage
    The world's great light ; the surging waves o'er
        sweep
The best wrought deed of mind, of warrior, sage :
    With cruel joy the barbarous gleaners reap.
Athena, from her god-abiding rock,
    Lifts up her tearful eyes, and lifts to see
Her sister, fair Corinthus, meet the shock ;
    But looks in vain—the spoilers hear no plea.—
Go, tell, Æolus, in thy wingéd flight,
How Hellas' day has changed to endless night !

THE PLEDGE.

GOOD friend, and wilt thou say,
 When this, my presence, here shall
   coldly lie,
  That in this still, lone way
 Thy feet, by fondest intuition, oft
   shall hie;
 E'en tho' I be not here—and know
   well why?

  Nay, stay that glistening tear!
'Twas but my thought of what—ah! what may be;
  'Twas breathed, for thou art near;
My thought led awe afar, then back to thee
Unfettered came—save with my heart's one plea.

  See this unprospered flower!
The dawn's glad salutation saw it blithe and fair.
  'Tis eve's young hour;
Some churlish hand hath left its impress there.
Mayhap, so unforeseen, my own sad share.

  Say such be death's acquest.
If, for my bosom, I thy vow achieve,
  And for thine—my behest;
If thou wilt of me fondest thoughts unreave,
His mandate come—I'll hence—nor idly grieve.

  And, when I pass away,
Thou'lt seek my semblance in some friend of
   thine;
  And with him here thou'lt stray;
Teaching, with sweetest intonation, that was mine,
That he may, when thou sleep'st, our names
   intwine.

ALONG THE STREAM.

THIS is the bubbling, laughing brook.
 Recall that wanton summer day
When we harassing care forsook,
 And woo'd its lone, meandering way.
How like some blended, fading dream,
The day we fared along the stream!

And here the gaily mottled bank!
 Some fate each nodding daisy said
When thou, fair priestess Vesta, sank
 And I assumed assent or pled.
How real, yet how perverse, now seem
Our fancies told along the stream!

'Twas here we wove the royal crown,
　　O'er-studded from our perfumed store ;
And, for bright jewels, sought adown
　　Where on its breast our brooklet bore
Great gems : Did Indus of the Treasure deem
Her realm outshone along this stream ?

Here, we the harmless ford essayed :
　　But then how harmful it appeared !
How coyly did'st enjoin—delayed
　　To tempt its hurrying course ; and feared
To ope thy tenderest eyes, whose gleam
O'er-tided him who spann'd the stream.

Yes ! 'tis the gurgling, bubbling brook.
　　Soon, soon 'twill be the placid river.
Keep in thy heart our fair-day look—
　　My happiest day — and thou the giver.
How like a cherished, fadeless dream—
The day we fared along the stream !

MESSAGES.

WHAT is the song the Oriole sings,
    As she wings—as she wings?
My home to the loftiest bough shall
      hold,—
    For my note is harsh and none will
      heed,—
    That afar may be seen my vestment of
      gold;
For who so gorgeous in wood or mead?
    This is the message the Oriole brings,
    As away to her swinging home she wings.

    What is the song the Linnet sings,
      As she wings—as she wings?
My note's of the sweetest; my heart is warm;
    I can brook no fetter; the hawthorn hedge
Is my sunshine home; for the wintry storm
    I haste with my mates to the glad sea's edge!
      This is the message the Linnet brings,
      As away to her perfumed home she wings.

    What is the song the Cuckoo sings,
      As she wings—as she wings?
I have found me a home in some borrowed nest;
    I'll away and proclaim a warning call

With a clamorous note from my swelling breast—
　　The bright-bowed torrent that soon must fall!
　　　This is the message the Cuckoo brings,
　　　As away o'er the ripening harvest she wings.

　　　What is the song the Mead-lark sings,
　　　　As she wings—as she wings?
My home with a joyous cry I gain:
　　Of all I have chosen the meadow's brink;
And my fledgelings sport down the shadowy lane,
　　And the odorous spray of the wild-thyme drink!
　　　This is the message the Mead-lark brings,
　　　As over the waving meadow she wings.

　　　What is the song the Redstart sings,
　　　　As she wings—as she wings?
I must tell you my secret as hence I fly
　　To practice my arts in the wood away;
Tho' few bear such manifold charms as I,
　　No moment I find for their idle display!
　　　This is the message the Redstart brings,
　　　As away to the moss-grown beech she wings.

　　　What is the song the Blackbird sings,
　　　　As she wings—as she wings?
In the lonely wood, in a plaintive tone
　　Of deep, pure warblings, I breathe my tale

To my listening mate ; then he carols alone,
   And with answering echo gladdens the vale !
      This is the message the Blackbird brings,
         As away to the darkening thicket she wings.

      What is the song the brown Thrush sings,
         As she wings—as she wings ?
At morn and at eve shall your heart be stirred,
   For who so hears it will love my song ;
By day I must hide where the rivulet's heard,
   In my favorite haunt, as it pours along !
      This is the message the brown Thrush brings,
         As away to her shaded hollow she wings.

      What is the song the Redbreast sings,
         As she wings—as she wings ?
Who follows the path of the blast so soon,
   Or lingers so long on the crimson crest ?
My strain can the haughtiest passion attune
   To the peaceful lay of my loving breast !
      This is the message the Redbreast brings,
         As away to her mapled bower she wings.

      What is the song the Mock-bird sings,
         As she wings—as she wings ?
I have stolen a strain from each carolling throat,—
   Since few will list to my tuneless voice,—

And I mingle a sigh with the lover's note,
   Or I make from the resonant forest my choice!
     This is the message the Mock-bird brings,
    As away on her studious flight she wings.

    What is the song my Spirit sings,
      As it wings—as it wings?
I will seek some spot by a woodland slope,
   Till the shining sun to his rest shall wend,
And then I will tell a sweet thought and hope
   To the hark'ning ear of each pluméd friend!
    This is the message my Spirit brings—
     And its timorous flight to the future wings.

THE FOG-BELL.

THE fog-bell! The fog-bell!
   List, as its rhythmic measures swell!
The bell hangs by the castle moat
   That all who, wandering, as they near,
May catch its accents as they float,—
   Soothing with hope each anxious fear,—
That all may heed it well.

The fog-bell! The fog-bell!
   I've wondered whence its subtle spell:
For oft, as lengthening shadows lay,
   I've mused (where it securely swung,
Nor sped its warning tones away)
   Upon its mute, and senseless tongue,—
   Nor need to heed it well.

The fog-bell! The fog-bell!
   The weary captive in his cell
Hears it; and knows the world without
   Is shrouded in relentless mist,—
Immersed with his sad soul in doubt,—
   And he, unseen, its thought dismissed.
   Poor captive, heed it well!

The fog-bell! The fog-bell!
The busy house-wife's thought will dwell
While yet she holds her irksome round ;
  And, as its quavers loiter there
She rests apart, and to its sound
  She joins her homely, unfeigned prayer.
    Good house-wife, heed it well!

The fog-bell! The fog-bell!
How oft the storm-tossed sailor's knell!
Long, rude days past the hand, so skilled,
  Has guided on, from farthest climes:
Fond visions that his bosom thrilled
  Fade with its dreaded, funeral chimes.
    Brave sailor, heed it well!

The fog-bell! The fog-bell!
May it another message tell?
An idler sought the shore's lone waste
  With no concern, save careless thought:
He turned him thence, his heart o'ertraced
  With precepts that the fog-bell taught.—
    Kind idler, heed them well!

THE DEATH OF THE ORIOLE.

WE mourned him by the oak-land way,
   At wandering time thro' field and wold,
Where in his loveliness he lay,
   His music-breathing bosom—cold.

What need? why should the hunter's shaft
Make such the victim of its blight?
Who dreamed a zephyr's breath could waft
So dread a missile in its flight?

Poor, injured birdling, we deplore
Thy timeless fate! Thy part in life
Was through cerulean realms to soar,
Apart from this unheedful strife.

What lowly object here of harm
With specious pleadings won thine eye?
To teach thee for thy every charm
The world's return to thee—to die.

Wouldst not, if mightst, poor wanderer, say
Of those whose refuge was thy breast?
Bereft, in some deep vale—away,
Some vale of Tempe—pure and blest.

And, how may he, whose hurtful hand
Could spoil them of their birthright dower,
Presume, when he too nears the strand,
To ask the tokens of His power

For those whose accents are his joy,
With smiles responsive to his own?
And, for their sure defence, employ
The parting suppliant's anxious tone?

THEODORA.

THE bell proclaims the race.
  A potent monarch's heart again rebounds;
Ten thousand echoing voices swell the
    sounds;
  And joy illumes each face.
On all-impatient steeds, in bright array,
Byzantium's maids encounter for the
    fray.

He sees them waiting stand
For that soft sound that bids them swiftly fly;

He marks but one sweet face with drooping eye,—
    She curbs with trembling hand.
It seems amiss that her young, gentle life
Should find its place in this deep, maddening strife.

    Now, to their task they spring;
And onward, o'er the course a whirlwind rushing,
While thunders roll around, Hope Fear is hushing;
    For as the echoes ring
To joyful shouts, he heeds but that brave crest
That tells a timid maid leads all the rest.

    On to the goal they speed!
With mighty stride each supple steed is leaping.
With mighty throbs one heart in time is keeping.
    Will victory end the deed?
Appalling sight! she sinks, nor hears the storm;—
Down in the dust there lies a pale, fair form!

    Whence came that ardent plea?
From him who sits the throne, imperial, proud;
From him o'er yon bewondered Cypriot bowed;
    From heart of royalty.
He lifts her from the dust, ignoble, lone.—
She shares the state majestic—shares the throne!

THE CAPE OF STORMS.

REST thee, thou rambler o'er life's sea!
Some counsel with thee I would seek:
For surely thou mayst whisper me
Of that far region, dark and bleak,
Of circling pools and shattered forms—
Yet all-seductive Cape of Storms.

Aye, once I viewed that hostile peak,
That promontory's deep scarred side;
I caught its dismal whirlwind's shriek
And heard its caverns wail, deride;
And favored is the bark that 'scapes
That fatal, stormiest of the capes!

But say its raging mood were stilled;
That ocean calmer aspects lent;
That kind, propelling breezes filled
The wings by many a tempest bent;
If then his course he deftly shape
Might he not round that stormiest cape?

No hope! Forbearance is the snare
By which is stored its sateless rift;
Fallacious hopes soft breezes bear
Enshrouded in their flattering drift.

Soon its dissembling tones will teach
The terrors of that storm-strewed beach.

But, voyager, o'er those troubled tides
Perchance some spirit claims its sway,
And guilt in fairest presence hides
That those unversed shall surely stray;
Perchance, too, some rash rover's boast
Now wafts him toward that storm-marred coast?

E'en so. That fringed and ragged shore,
Told by yon headland lifted up,
Proclaims the fruit the vintage bore—
Tilled for the Spirit of the Cup.
Beware, O fair and cherished forms,
That all-seductive Cape of Storms!

THE RECLUSE.

Your hearts be for the recluse unoppressed!
Of all poor mortals calls he himself blessed.
On no splenetic humor builds his hope,
But infinite as nature is its scope;
Within his breast installs a trustiest friend
His every act to censure or commend;
And, too, each secret motive quick reviews.
Nor every slight indulgence misconstrues;
The worth and weight of action e'er computes,
Restrains excesses and his harm disputes;
Upholds some cherished phantom to his gaze,
And gives an unsought radiance to his ways,
And lustre to each homely duty lends—
Renewing ever while its glow expends.
Felicity like this—unquestioned, pure,
Devised by reason, fashioned to endure,
The wisdom of his choice seems to attest;
And leaves no untilled field for vain request.

Attend the recluse for his day's long round.
At dawn forth from his couch with joyful bound,
To welcome coming day. The god of sleep

Bids speed him hence his wasteful watch to keep
O'er those enthralled by his alluring reign,
Which, when confirmed, he ever will maintain.
Released from bondage, on he takes his flight,
Speeding the fading glories of the night;
Impatiently foretastes the lingering day—
Chiding the motive for its long delay.
A herald comes anon, in robes of state,
To speak the orb's approach—resplendent, great,
Who spreads o'er earth a glittering, jewelled
    band,—
The princely tokens of a royal hand,—
Ere yet he hasten on with generous stealth
To share with all his all-surpassing wealth.
On hies the wanderer in the happiest dawn;
Assumes as his the teachings of the morn;
Some clear-writ line perceives at every look,
Or takes some glad refrain from every brook.
Mayhap, his thought recalls some well-conned text
That at some time, 'long past, its course perplexed,
But now has learned its excellence so well
That though unsummoned—yet its tale will tell.
Thus on, till each accustomed trophy won,
He turns him homeward. See his day begun!

Now to his favorite haunt for dear converse—
The silent realm of theme prolix and terse

Traced o'er the living page.   Then, may awake
The long-stilled voice that there its bonds can
      break
To fetch the buried ages from the tomb,
To breathe their airy nothingness, and bloom
With rising monarchs, or with toppling king.
He views the swaying nations—hears the ring
Of myriad voices or the deep despair
Of him whose every prospect once was fair ;
The sanctimonious prelate and the saint
With holy pretence their vile deeds bepaint,—
Abjuring His commands who set them there,—
To claim with sensual courts, dominion's share ;
Or, their base passions on some land obtrude
Till loathsome things proclaim its solitude :
While their names shine with proud prefix adorned,
And praises said to those whom Honor scorned.
But these are forms far banished to the past—
The darkening clouds that sunlit skies o'ercast ;
The dull, mean clods the beauteous gem withhold,
Which, once removed, its virtues more unfold.
A mighty phalanx stand the good and pure,
Whose fair, ennobling tenets shall endure
Till earth and heaven be aged : these shall he call
To peaceful consultation.   If befall
A mood to sorrow, profit, or to please,
He'll find some spirit with that mood agrees.

The day has flown, and, 'tis the cherished hour:
He strays afar, beneath the sky-pierced bower,
And feels how poor and lowly is his place
When measured by the endless span of space.
From yon etherial, vasty realm afar,
There comes a wearied ray: 'tis from a star
By sweet Urania named. It murmurs not,
Because, forsooth, it seemed an unkind lot
To set so fair an orb so deep in gloom
To, innocently, expiate some doom;
And those who've met its lone, estrangéd ray,
Aver none purer in yon jeweled way.

Worldling! ere thou adjudge the recluse' fate,
Take to thy heart that absent wanderer's state.

ALCIBIADES' SOLILOQUY.

[Alcibiades, at the request of his grateful countrymen, leaves the scene of his successes in the East, and turns his trireme homewards. The night before the anticipated arrival at the port of Piræus, he reclines thoughtfully at the prow, gazing into the moonlit waters; while his heart is alternately filled with joy at his present prosperity, and depressed with doubts, when he reflects that perhaps the calamitous Sicilian expedition and its consequences are too well remembered.]

SLEEP, my suggestive soul! nor longer force
   The vexious labyrinth of years misspent!
   Or, since thou wilt unsummoned yet discourse,
   Let thy swift footsteps seek some happier bent.
Why shoulst not thou, as yon great orb of day,
Sink thy all-ruling state and find thy rest?
Than thou more kind, he will not ever sway,
But woos repose in fair Argolis' breast;
Whilst thou, poor imitator of his prudent might,
Art not content to cast thy sceptre down

And grant thy weary subject a respite.
Why wilt thou stay Oblivion's gloom, and chain
    my deeds to light?

My fate the morrow's certainty unfolds!
O Intimation, canst thou speak that fate?
That, as the future's speechless veil uprolls,
Unwonted pride may not this heart elate,
Or deep emotions to quick eyes attest
Its crowning passion. In my hungering ear,
That waits impatiently the banquet blest,
Is it decreed that happiest throngs shall pour
The loud acclaim ; or, shall I once more hear
The fatal murmurs of Charybdis' shore
That rests unmoved as to its rude embrace
The winsome tide bears on the bark that soon no
    eye may trace?

And thou, broad, restless Ægean! e'en thy might,
Subdued by pale Diana's countless shafts,
Would say how Hope may pierce thro' Doubt's
    dark night,
To cheer the bark some blessed promise wafts
On to its haven. Yon bright pathway's gleam,—
Fair harbinger of glory's rapturous way,—
Would guide aright my proud, ambitious dream,
And Retribution's stern alarms allay.

In the abyss this dark wide waste upbears,
Forever let Suspicion's impulse stray:
Whilst I, unshackled from o'er-pressing cares,
Now gaze into its depths profound and crave the
    peace it shares.

Yet painting e'er that day of joy and dread
When the majestic fleet lost Piræus' wall
And to Sicilian waters onward sped?
Or dwellest thou on Athena's sacred call?
The deep revenge my raging bosom planned;
Then to the foe to seal my country's doom;
On to the haughty monarch's breadthless land;
There to entreat my birthright's deathless gloom?
True, reason came with power to attain
Its lost possession, and its reign assume,
There to abide and hide the monstrous stain.—
Say yon inconstant city's voice adjudge that com-
    pact vain!

Oh! let my feet th' inspiring bema press,
Where eloquence so oft usurped my tongue!—
How yearned my heart its passion to caress,
When all unheard for Hermæ's crime 'twas wrung!
Wrong shall be banished. Right shall claim her
    own;
And he who from the state's injustice fled

Shall win his country's praise,—in sweetest tone
From him who first condemned. For who hath led
Her fleet triumphant? Who hath ranged the band
'Neath the proud banner? These my cause have
    pled.
On, then, brave steed by Ægean zephyrs fanned!
On, then, brave soul, fear not the voice of thine
    auspicious land!

ECHO.

EEP in the woodland glade
  Comes Juno's laughing maid,
    Now sorrow-blighted;
  No sportive pastime telling;
  The crystal jewels welling
    That joy once lighted.

With frown, from Atthis' land,
Nemesis, with her wand,
    Too, counselling with her;
Till thro' the wild-wood winging

ECHO.

Sweet Echo's tones are ringing—
    Then hastening thither

To where the fount is sleeping,
A secret vigil keeping
    For him comes speeding
Uncared; the bright hours wiling;
With blithesome note beguiling—
    His fate unheeding.

Enchained by mystic link,
To the reflective brink
    The goddess guides him:
He sighs, he dies—adoring;
The limpid shade imploring
    That in it hides him!

And there a floweret clings.
A saddening tale it brings;
    Or, task assuming,
It bears the lover warning,
To love, no longer scorning
    Narcissus blooming.

AYESHA.
(Seventh Century.)

AYESHA, when the dread sand-sea
   Us its billow rolls between,
Guard, with sometime thought for me,
   This fair rose of Damascene.

Share with it the dawn's first thought;
   Forth, when Orient's splendors rise!
Haste thee, that its sense be taught
   Glories more than his—thine eyes.

By thee, 'neath the fervid ray,
   Be its drooping form o'erdewed:
So its lapsing life may stay,
   To enduring beauty wooed.

And when evening shades appear,
   Linger, that in loneliness
Fancy's bodings, phantomed near,
   Ne'er its fainting strength oppress.

Then, should words of kind intent
   O'er its state from thee outpour,
Blessed as cry of muezzin sent
   To Natolia's faithful shore

Comes then, hastening, Ayesha's sigh,
  Saying, Nay! thy heart's true queen
Kinder, since thou art not by,
  Lov'st thy rose of Damascene!

TO PHILOMEL.

(From the French.)

WHY wilt thou, plaintive Philomel,
  Ne'er from thy sorrow seek relief?
  To me, who come to share thy grief,
To me thy heart's emotion tell.

The universe, in brightest shades,
  Presents her beauties to beguile;
  The bowered Dryads hope with smile
To woo thee onward to their glades.

Afar the Northwind's breath expires,
  And thrusts aside his chilling cares;
  The Earth her verdured mantle wears;
The sky's aglow with beauteous fires!

For you Cephalus' love presumes
　　With diamonds Flora to o'erspray ;
　　While Zephyr seizes on his way
Earth's wanton store of rare perfumes.

The birds have ceased their warbling-strife
　　To catch again thy sad refrain ;
　　The hunter stays his hand again,
Nor thinks to mar thy guileless life.

Yet in thy tortured bosom dwell
　　The luckless shafts to Fortune left,
　　When one a sister's heart had cleft—
So cruelly she aimed—and well !

Alas ! could my sad thought persuade
　　The healing past into my heart !
　　Thy griefs are robed with memory's art,
By present hours are mine arrayed.

Thy griefs, when Nature quick espies,
　　She soothes with fairest prospect spread ;
　　Mine are in poignant regions led,
Where envious Present stops my sighs.

BERENICE.

BLOW, thou churlish ice-wind, blow!
    Beat, ye angry tempests, beat!
With ceaseless dashings, torrents, flow!
    Think ye to stay his hastening feet?
What heeds my brave love, for his step is light;
And eyes would be dimmed came he not to-night.

Fly, O drift-wind, over the moor,
    Moaning tales of a gloomy heath,
Of a faithless track, of a raiment pure,
    A silent sleep and eddied wreath.
Nay, 'twill stay him not in his eager flight,
For roses would fade came he not to-night.

Remorseful boughs, be ye lifted high:
    Bespeak my love, for he long delays.
Pants he ever on? dost thou know his cry?
    Hath he sunk to rest in the wild moor-maze?
If my love be bound in a cerement white,
Low, heart, lie thee low on the moor to-night!

ETHEL.

(Daughter of Edwin and Julia.)

BEMOANING her? Ah, nay!
   'Twas the good Master called.
   She heard, and, unappalled
Nor sought, nor wished delay.
   Oh, unsubmissive deed!
   Relentlessly to plead
To hear the voice that, echoing, died away.

Stayed not. Down to the strand
   With holy impulse came,
   Whilst yet her breathed name
Was said to the pure band;
   Their joyous voices told
   How she, to greet the fold,
Need trustingly but touch their Saviour's hand.

Darkly the torrent swept.
   She faltered at its brink—
   Angel, skilled but to think
How shining ways are kept!—
   He saw her heart distressed,
   And onward swiftly pressed,—
She, from his bosom, saw its flood o'erstept.

With deep solicitude
    She reads his face divine;
    But haply notes no sign
How sufferings may intrude.
    Forever freed from pain:
    Unpitying wish—and vain,
That she should share our hours with pains
    imbued.

ON CONCLUDING CICERO'S SIXTH PHILLIPIC.

O LIBERTY, poor flickering dying flame !
  O breath of Eloquence, whose flames endure !
O once proud substance ! now a sounded name ;
  O light of nations ! gleaming, ever pure.

ON CONCLUDING THE FIFTH VOLUME OF GIBBON'S "DECLINE AND FALL OF THE ROMAN EMPIRE."

I CLOSE thee, volume, with a pang—and joy,
  A pang at banishment from Moslem, Greek :
Rejoicing I may yet my thought employ
  With deeds and heroes future pages speak.

PAUSANIAS.

DRAMATIS PERSONÆ.

PAUSANIAS, *a Spartan General.*
TISAMENUS, *a Diviner.*
LYDUS, *a boy attending Pausanias.*

SCENES—The Camp at Platæa, then at Byzantium, and lastly near Sparta.

SCENE I.—*Platæa. A camp at night.*

Enter PAUSANIAS.

PAU. Another day has gone,
And silent night has curtained o'er our host.
My soul hath made resolve, ere Phœbus' car
Shall toil the brow of high Cithæron's mount,
The haughty foe shall taste our weighty steel,
And turn him hence in ignominious haste;
Or Sparta's sons shall take that longest rest.
Lydus, attend!

Enter LYDUS.

LYDUS. Here, lord, to do your pleasure.
PAU. My gentle helot, didst thou not relate,

In sportive manner for thy comrade's ear,
How Elea's prophet came into our camp
In soiled attire, and rests with thoughtful mien
Within its limit?

    LYD. 'Tis true, my lord. It was but yester
        eve, —
The wakeful sentry kept his anxious watch
To see the heavy hours creep slowly by, —
When, as yon star that doth the west inflame
Had sunk to rest, there came, as from the gloom,
A halting figure. Nothing would it speak
Save, properly, the word that doth insure
Our camp's repose and surety 'gainst the foe.
Him thus the sentry willed to pass him by,
And saw him brooding by the cheerful fire
Whilst all the phalanx courted soothing sleep.
There kept he in that same strange attitude,
When I, at early morn by sleep renewed,
Did seek my duties. I did him long observe;
And from my musings wove a jesting tale
To tell my comrades: how from Pluto's realm
A cunning spirit had by trick obtained
The key that doth unlock the nether world,
And fled to earth. It was this tale you heard.
If it doth give offense, your pardon on it.

    PAU. Nay, boy, it matters not. I rather joy
That thou hast pleasant humor. Canst thou tell

His name and present business?

Lyd. He is a seer, and doth of fate forecast;
His name, Tisamenus.

Pau. Seek him e'en to the camp's extremest
verge;
Tell him that Sparta's valiant captain waits,
And would hold converse.

Lyd. This will I do and come with much dispatch. [*Exeunt.*

Pau. Now may I know the issue of our trials;
The great events that by them shall declare.
Perchance the tongues of ages yet to be
Shall sound our glories on to infant ears,
And each shall sigh, that destiny had willed
Long years of intervention. Perchance a shade
As deep in hue as that o'er Stygian flood
Shall blight this happy land, and time shall weep
And shudder as it ponders! Lydus draws near,
In quick attendance on the thoughtful seer.

Enter Tisamenus; Lydus *keeps the door.*

Welcome, good friend, if haply so you prove.
Yon harmless boy of thee hath brought report,
Whose strange complexion bids me seize a hope
That thou mayst argue from some secret sign
The fruitful morrow, and what swift result
Shall crown its dreadful conflict. Tell me this.

Tis. Dost thou know me?
Pau. Thy name I know, and 'tis Tisamenus.
Tis. Canst build the structure of thy hopes and
    fears
        On such foundation?
Pau. There is a gift by mighty Zeus willed
To live and mingle in the royal blood
Of Sparta's kings. Such is this potent gift
That he can read, as with the stycale's rod,
The thought that flits portrayed upon each face:
And by this mean I know thy hidden powers.
Such is the virtue of it.
  Tis. Mine is a gift that far outmatches thine.
In my fair youth Elea was my state,
Where, with the swains, the Hyblæan brood I
    chased;
Till with ennobling years proud visions came,
And thirsts for emulation. Thence away
The Pythian's blessing to obtain; then ask
Her much sought counsel. Her, with great
    amaze,
I heard pronounce a fate of much import:
That in five contests I should victor be.
No more she'd speak, but I must time abide
To learn their nature. Yet it hath not been.
To the Olympic sand from Andros came
One who o'erthrew me in the heated strife.

It seemeth then my triumphs must be won
Upon the bloody field : my gleaming sword
Shall hurl yon myrmidons back to their haunts.

    Pau. But, sir, what of thy rare prophetic gift?
It is for that I bade thee to my tent.

    Tis. She that endowed me with my blessed
        hope
Did grant a blessing that doth it excel,—
Breathing into my soul a subtle power
Whereby such things as have not yet seen life
Stand forth apparent. This I'll not impart
Save for a compensation men adjudge
Beyond compare. O Spartan, hear thou it :
To be a fellow of thy honored state
Is my desire. Attain this by thy speech :
To all thy wishes will I then comply ;
And we, in unison, will teach the foe
What virtues dwell in heroes.

    Pau. I'll to our generals, and tell them all.
Stay ! I will soon return. Lydus, away !
                                      [*Exeunt.*

    Tis. This Spartan, though a bold one, and
        approved,
Hath that within him that may well be spared :
It is the calm that tempts the nautilus !
The exigencies that enshroud this time
Have forced him to the near regards of men :

But, when the time of blissful peace shall come,
This rigid oak, that bows not to the wind,
Shall, by the flame insidious luxury fans,
O'er topple in its pride—and shake the earth.
But soft! he comes again—and all assent.

Enter PAUSANIAS, *Ephors, Generals and Soldiers.*

PAU. Tisamenus, much is your point discussed,
And many think your price too much enhanced.
But, terror of the Median host is such
That all do yield; and do their hopes intrust
To the joined honors of our several hearts.
What say you of our chances?

TIS. For this great honor I do give you thanks;
And I shall so comport my every act
To bring a happy issue to our perils.
Spartans, know this: Yon river that divides
The gorgeous host from our too eager band
Would stay your course. Across the turbid tide
Lurk many dangers. So, e'en to our foe
Come he to this. We will await him here.
Asopus dared, his folly shall appear!

Scene II.—*Byzantium.*—Pausanias, *in a Persian robe, banqueting in great magnificence, surrounded by his officers.*—*Music.*

Pau. Slaves! be ye still, and list to my command.
Fill with the ruby wine each sparkling cup!
Ha! Ha! thought we along Asopus' side
That night could ever witness sight like this?
Lydus, thou dog, come hence! What was my speech
When we then dreamed among our foes and spoils?

Lydus. You bade our Grecian officers attend:
You'd have them see, you said, the Persian's folly;
And marvelled he should leave his prosperous home
To wrench a homely pittance from our hearths:
You bade the helots pile the massy spoil
On countless beasts of strange and unknown mould,
And bear it thence to many a sacred shrine:
You then bade spread our humble, frugal fare,—
In mighty contrast to the Persian's pomp,—
And said the lesson that it did avouch
Was, that by modest mien and honor's path
Men are ordained for freedom:—Save your hand!

PAU. Nay, fool, I will not strike;—tell on your
    tale.
LYD. But, since your brain hath turned with
    glory's pomp;
Since you despise what you did then commend,
Your friends have from you one by one far flown,
Till you are, like Laocoon, all entwined
Within the lawless pleasures of this court.
I crave thy pardon. Thou didst bid me speak.
  PAU. Out, villian, and call hence Tisamenus!
                              [*Exit* LYDUS.
That vile imposter who himself withholds,
Thinking to check our mirth and pleasant hours;
Giving himself much praise, because forsooth
Some actions he foretold went not amiss.

            Enter TISAMENUS.

Well, citizen, how fares it with thee now?
Dost think the price once paid for thy fair words
Was gain to Sparta?
  TIS. For my poor coin great riches I have
    gained;
The gain to Sparta may not thus allow.
  PAU. Put off thy riddling and speak plainly
    now.
  TIS. 'Twas my ill fortune, one brief year ago,
To own a state that could no honors boast;

But now o'er happiest Sparta may I roam,
As her proud son.
    PAU. Know, proud son, thine is a matron
        gauded.
Of that pertains to riches she hath not:
She hath a boundless store of arrogance:
Nought else besides.
    TIS. Pausanias, thou shalt perforce hear me.
Thou art the sorriest wreck of all these times.
Like great Diana thou didst climb the sky;
And like her thou art sinking—all but shorn.
I tell thee, man, that Sparta marks thy crime:
She knows thy wild intents—thy hopes shall die.
What means this aping of her deadliest foe?
Thy flowing robes, rich collars, fragrant wines?
What means this tale the guardian winds bear
        her?
To wed the monarch's daughter thou wouldst
        give
Him all domain?—and, can it then be
That thing so base had birth on Sparta's soil?
I tell thee, madman, how thy sun has set:
Thy country's summons stays but at the door.—
Ho! guards, attend, and bear this traitor hence!

   [*Enter guards who bind* PAUSANIAS *and exeunt.*

SCENE III.—*Sparta, near the Temple, in Minerva's Grove.*

Enter PAUSANIAS, *disguised. A boy disguised.*

PAU. Tell me, good Lydus, is't not by this wood
That great Minerva keeps her solemn state?
　LYD. Methinks we should be near it.
　PAU. O dreadful bolt that rived yon knotty oak!
Why dost thou pass me by to vent thy spleen
On that which gladdens nature? Why blast there
And I stand by unharmed? O Jupiter,
Send thy shaft next into this hateful breast—
This life detestable! Ope now thy hand!
Oft have I viewed the hurrying lightning's play,
And heard Jove's thunders sounded earth around
In breathless wonderment. Boy, fearest thou not?
When I was of thy fresh and tender age,
'Twas of all deeds most fearful: wiser grown
The fancies of that age yet ever stayed.
Using that expedition it retains,
It cannot now break through this wall too soon!
　LYD. I pray thee, that thou shouldst not yet despair.

There are such shiftings in this world of ours
That Fortune's gifts lie strewed upon our paths
Where least expected. Bid thy courage up!
Here is the Temple: we will fly to it.
And, dying at Minerva's feet, thus gain
Immortal honors elsewhere sought in vain!

Enter citizens who wall the entrances to the Temple.

CANST THOU FORGET?

CANST thou forget? Ah, say 'tis joyous spring,
  Green every field, and rustling every bower.
  No song save thine can sweetest songster bring;
    No voice save thine can waken every flower.
The harebell thus: Why, fondest, stayest thou yet?
  Dost think then, harebell, that we can—forget?

Canst thou forget? Ah, say 'tis summer come.
  We woo, outstretched, the shriveling stream, whose note

Makes harmony with restless insects' hum,
　　And fancies shape where fleecy atoms float:
Yon structure bold is fair—none fairer, yet
　　'Twas planned for thee. Dost think we can—
　　　　forget?

Canst thou forget? Ah, say 'tis autumn, dyed
　　And trophied o'er with deep-hued leaf and tree.
We turn afield—then stay, for one beside:
　　Mem'ry's illusion, fondest, 'twas for thee!
Apart, with oft-communings, stores we set,
　　Full for thy sake. How canst thou say—forget?

Canst thou forget? Ah, say 'tis winter drear.
　　We mutely stray, that Nature may not wake;
We stoop and flaked trac'ries now appear.
　　Wouldst know the characters our musings
　　　　make?
A name. Why, fondest, this is thine! this yet!
　　For hearts guide hands. Dost think we can—
　　　　forget?

Canst thou forget? Aye, when yon matchless
　　　　light
　　Forgets to gleam far into ether-space!
It shall be then thou'lt fade from memory's sight,
　　Then cease to phantom each familiar place.
Thy doubt hath wronged us, fondest: never yet,—
Mine eyes are dark'ning,—need to say—forget.

INVITATION TO ÆNEAS TO TARRY AT DELOS.

'TIS of Delos we sing, of the bride of the
    waters,
  Haply set on the crest of the soft
    Ægean wave;
 How joyous the strain when Mnemo-
    syne's daughters
  Sing of Delos, whose footstool the blue
    waters lave!

See! all Cyclades stand as in haste to embrace it:
  'Tis to lovingly shield it from Boreas' wiles.
They his keen blasts have kept, that its charms
    ever grace it;
  By them borne his frowns, for it treasured his
    smiles.

Aphrodite's bold son, shun Ausonia's dominions,
  Where the swords now unsheathed to bright
    bucklers resound;
Let thy flying steed rest, folded be her broad
    pinions,—
  'Tis for thee at fair Delos the banquet is
    crowned.

Harpies eye thee askance, fell Cyclopean strangers
  Now would wave thee to isles favored, seemingly fair;
Troubles lurk in their groves, in their atmosphere dangers,
  And the sirens are false as the smile that they wear.

The brazen beak turns not; cruel Fate him empowers.
  On, then, tempt Sidon's queen with illusive delights!
O most god-like of men, borne from Ilium's towers,
  Why range the seas longer when Delos invites?

THE TWILIGHT HOUR.

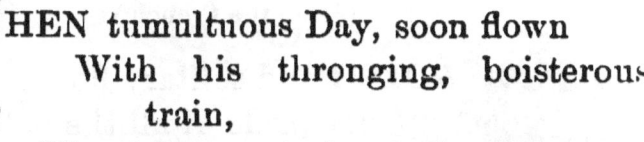HEN tumultuous Day, soon flown
    With his thronging, boisterous train,
Wrapt in roseate-hued disguise,
    Paints the sky with daintiest stain,
When the gentle zephyrs rise,
    Be that hour thine own.

'Tis the hour of calm repose ;
    Tranquil influences breathe ;
Then each passion sinks to rest,
    And Hope's frailest tendril-wreath,
Crushed till then within the breast,
    Upward coyly grows.

Unimpassioned, thou'lt review
    Many a heedless word outspoken ;
Deeds that then seem veriest madness ;
    Tenderest friendship all but broken ;
And once more, with sense of sadness,
    All thy vows renew.

Watch through twilight's soft decline ;
    See the future's thread unroll'd ;
Keep the hour that seemeth lonely—
    'Twill to thee thy worth unfold :
Fellowship'd with conscience only,
    Guard that hour as thine.

LA FLEUR.

(From the French.)

FADING and solitary flower,
   Once pride of all the dale,
Behold thy dower with ruthless
      power
   Dispelled by every gale!

   Fate thus from many a mortal reaps,—
We're kindred save in name,—
A zephyr sweeps, the leaflet leaps—
   Past pleasure whilst it came.

Each day that lingers with the past
   Some cherished dream enfolds;
'Twas fairly cast; yet, like the last,
   A fancied dream withholds.

Till wondering mortals, stirred by grief
   At retrospective hours,
Ask why, beneath, is life so brief
   To ecstacy and flowers?

LINES TO THE ALABAMA RIVER.

FLOW on, mysterious torrent, by the might
   That taught thee first to thread yon deep recess ;
Roll onward in thy stern and sluggish flight,—
   Toward ocean press.

Perchance some crystal lakelet was the source
   From whence thy life was drawn, with murmuring tone,
Unheedful of a future's tortuous course—
   So vast, so lone !

Impatient then in all thy glimmering length,
   Didst thou not scorn thy toils, as oft waylaid
Some noisome fen usurped thy lusty strength—
   Else festooned glade ?

Yet onward surged : their destinies enhance
   Thy murky volume by a near embrace ;
Then onward flow'd through Forest's still expanse
   With faltering pace.

To know thee first beneath the breathless night !
   How solemn, how unpitying, dost thou seem :

Again to view thee by the glittering light,
   Or mellowest beam!

And note the changeful shapes its rays entice;
   The weird phantasms that thy currents yield.
E'en thus, methinks, with many a quaint device
   Glow'd Thetis' shield.

As Oceanus there in wide confine
   Shut in the varied tale of valorous deeds,
So dark magnolia's form thou mayst divine
   Midst quivering reeds.

Flow on, O Alabama, by the might
   That won to thee this deadly wilderness!
None shall dispute with thee a sovereign's right
   Here to oppress!

   Mobile.

THE COMPLAINT.
(After "La Feuille" of Arnault.)

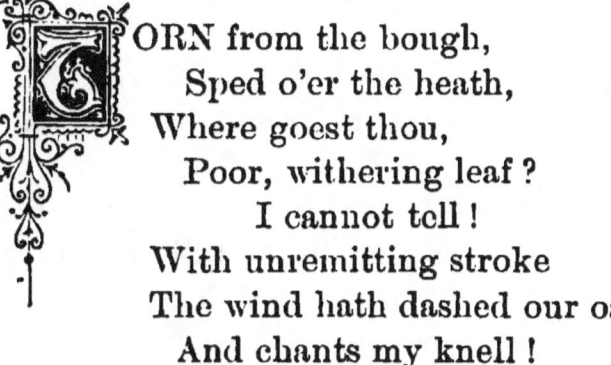ORN from the bough,
   Sped o'er the heath,
Where goest thou,
   Poor, withering leaf?
     I cannot tell!
With unremitting stroke
The wind hath dashed our oak,
   And chants my knell!

Soon life shall cease;
   Now here, now there,
At his caprice
   Borne on the air,
To plead were vain.
Submissively I sweep
By mountain top, or creep
   Low in the plain!

E'er thus to be?
   Unsparing lot!
Nor rest for me?
   O, breathe it not!
As I must all—
The humblest herb that blows,
Dark laurel, fragrant rose,
   Untimely fall?

LITTLE MAID OF ANGLESEY.

(Welsh Ballad.)

ITTLE maid of Anglesey,
How dream-like now it seems to me!
*　　*　　*　　*　　*

Behind, the evening vesper toll'd;
Before, the Biscan billow roll'd;
And I was borne to lands unknown,
And you were left to weep—alone.

Little maid of Anglesey,
From far adown the western sky
There came a messenger to me:
It was a last, a lingering tie;
It was that band of molten gold,
   Just blending with the shades of night,
Reflected from thy tresses, told
   Who watched—a farewell, signal light.

Little maid of Anglesey,
My heart that eve was full of thee:
For when that beacon ceased its flame
A thousand grateful memories came
From days bygone; and, pondering long
Bowed down, I met the gathering throng.
I viewed again the tapering spire;

I caught the accents of the choir;
The master's word, the near appeal,
(How oft the errant eye would steal
To one who listened at my side,
With holiest impulses to guide!)
The little cot, the rose-wreathed door,
The hill-side path, the oft-trod shore;
The evening pastime on the green—
I lived them o'er—each treasured scene.

Little maid of Anglesey,
Fair maidens dwell in Normandy;
And eyes there be that swiftly glance,
   And tones of softest breathings sigh,
And feet to merry measures dance
   Where full the yellow harvests lie.
I've met the glance to scorn its spell;
   The sigh passed as the idle wind:
I knew no lover's tale to tell,
   As through the mazy dance we twined.

Little maid of Anglesey,
Back, back the good ship came to thee.
My heart, my beating heart, was true;
And all its beatings as she flew,
Were that the lingering doubts of years
Might prove as idle as its fears;
And as she onward flew, and fast.

Again my eyes, as in the past,
This rock with eager questionings sought,
To know another ray had caught
Thy tresses gleam from out the night—
An ever-faithful, guiding light!

TO BROTHER.

WOULD, brother, would that ever thus
    Through life's uncertain weather,
Would it might ever be for us
    To wander on together!
Thus ever onward, side by side,
Thy voice to cheer, my hand to guide.

Would, brother, that thy kindly eye
    Might never beam less brightly!
Would that thy heart might ever lie
    Within its cell so lightly!
And be life's canopy to you
Thy cheek's own blushing, happy hue!

In glory walks our autumn-day,
    And faultless, to your reason ;
So, brother, be thy far-away—
    That ever-present season.
Be thus its by-ways broad and sure ;
    Above, its vapory realms as pure.

And if it be, for one, thine arm
    To point untrod direction ;
To shelter from a fancied harm—
    A brother's own protection.—
Then for him be that love of thine
As steadfast as for thee is mine !

THE FAILURE.

HANG out the red flag,
  (That ominous token
Of plans never realized,
  Contracts all broken)
Roll down the shutters;
  The occupant's fled
Where he heeds not anathemas
  Hurled at his head!
'Twas a desperate affray;
  And the wise self-debater
Saw fate must subdue him,
  Were it sooner or later.
He struggled in silence,
  No pang would reveal,
But ever an Ixion
  Writhed at the wheel.
What he did do was this,
  (And with reason enough),
He fled from the world—
  And the world's cold rebuff.

Now, down with his books—
  Let their pages be scanned!
Let us see how he ciphered,
  How reasoned and planned.

What a wonderful fabric
  Of unfinished scheming!
What a gossamer structure
  Of fanciful dreaming!
What a record of error!
  What a desperate showing!
What a pittance is due!
  What a mountain is owing!
Now on and yet on
  Staring characters stand;
First set, then erased
  With a tremulous hand,
With a wild throbbing brain
  And a quick beating pulse;
But the truth would remain
  With its changeless results!

So the books are far flung,
  And the tenant has flown.
But where did he go?
  Ah! that secret's his own.
Hand the calendar down!
  Add his name to the list!
From the world's busy train
  He's already dismiss'd!
But the eye, all-enchained,
  Now amazedly pauses;

What a blundering throng!
  What astonishing causes!
Read the record far up,
  To the top and the first,
And of all the disastrous
  This last is the worst!
This one toiled on for knowledge,
  Fed his hunger for learning;
For far-sounding plaudits,
  This failure was yearning;
This one grasped out for riches—
  And saw them depart;
This one played for a bubble—
  A cold, ashen heart;
This one tasted ambition—
  'Twas turmoil and strife:
But his was the saddest—
  The failure of life.

TELL ME, GOOD LADY-MOTHER, WHY.

TELL me, good Lady-mother, why
    The zephyr's laugh is still'd.
I like not its foreboding sigh,—
    My very heart is chill'd.
My child, the evening-breezes light,
Alarmed, fly the winds of night.

Tell me, good Lady-mother, why
    The gentle moonbeams fade.
Why should yon cloudlet hast'ning by
    Enfold them in its shade?
My child, a symbol 'tis, unfurled,
From storm-cloud to the zenith whirl'd.

Tell me, good Lady-mother, why
    The fitful gleam is near.
Its vivid dartings, flaming high,
    Oppress my heart with fear.
My child, it is the lightning's glare
Whose purity shall linger there.

Tell me, good Lady-mother, why
    So dark it seems—and strange.
Why lowers so the sparkling sky?

  I do not like the change.
My child, it is the blessed rain
That brighter makes the sky again.

  Tell me, good Lady-mother, why
   These smiles your features wreathe.
  Why falls the hand? why dims the eye?
   Is it the changeful eve?
Rains sobb'd; skies flamed in tempest wild—
Nor answer else came to the child.

SONNET.

(To my sister, with a copy of Shakespeare's Works.)

WHEN, from the varying phases of the mind,
  Thou'dst seek companionship for every mood,
  Open these pages, and behold enshrined
  A smile for gladness, tears for solitude.
  Within these narrow bounds thou'lt find, at best,
The subtlest strains the soul divine hath play'd—
What deep emotions told! what doubts express'd!
And every fault with just exactness weighed!
Call it a garden, blooming with sweet thought,
Whose true complexion serves but to inspire:
Within its pale each rarest flower is taught
To shed a fragrance that it holds entire.
So, if this garden thy quick sense attain,
Thou'lt fly all meads, and, craving, come again.

THE STAR OF FRIENDSHIP.

WHEN forth, again, upon the main
    The voy'ger tempts stern Ocean's
        wrath,
Though headland fade, yet, undismayed,
    He threads the crested path.

Nor fears; and why? There, gleaming
        high,
Behold the index to his way!
    When e'er he turns, there ever burns
That calm, celestial ray.

The Pole-Star's beam it is, whose gleam
    Emboldens all his fond desires:
He bounds the waste with ardent haste,
    If kindled be its fires.

Should, now, his bark through regions dark
    Pursue the Northwind to his lair,
'Twill upward rise, surmount the skies,
    And glow, yet purer, there.

If, now, the helm to sunniest realm
    The ever restive voy'ger brings,
It downward wends, with ocean blends,—
    Yet near to memory clings.

What though it sink beneath the brink
　　And perish to his earnest gaze?
He, wistful, sure, proclaims how pure,
　　How quenchless is its blaze!

Thus Friendship's star. It shines afar,
　　Assuring up life's treacherous zone:
Let climates smile, it lives the while
　　With constancy its own.

BELATED.

WHEN, wandering from his cherished nest,
The swallow seeks the needful rest
　　That thick'ning nightfall brings,
He, conscious of a watchful Power,
Forgets the darkness of the hour—
　　And folds his wearied wings.

Nor yet laments his home the less;
But sleeps, that he at dawn may press
　　On ere his loved one wake:
That when the gilded morn shall burst
He, of all eager songsters first,
　　His homeward flight may take.

THE CHANGING OF THE TIDES.

(At the rising of the tides the vessels float away into deep water, and the impatient fishermen diligently ply their vocation.)

    SLEEP no more! be true! comrades, awaken!
    The hour, so near the last, is full upon us!
    With loving arms the sea our bark hath taken:
    Let us make ours the fruit our watch hath won us.
To slumber now, fair fortune 'twere despising.
Then, comrades, up! the tide, the tide is rising!

    This weary stay our very hearts would sicken.
    How blest the time the waters are foretelling!
    If marked its healthful hue, your hearts will quicken;
    See how the limpid waves come ever swelling!
For us a harvest full they seem devising.
Then, comrades, up! the tide, the tide is rising!

    *   *   *   *   *   *

    O, cheerily, the harvest spreads before us!
    Forget, forget the hours of aimless leisure!
    Such hours as this to fortune must restore us;
    And to repletion hoard our bark with treasure.

'Twas for this golden hour our hearts were yearning.
Then, comrades, haste! the tide, the tide is turning!

  'Twill soon be gone—be gone past our availing.
    How deeply ever after would we sorrow!
  O, constant let us be, though strength seem failing:
    Our care shall vanish, joying on the morrow!
Bid all-allurements hence, with lofty spurning:
O comrades, toil! the tide, the tide is turning!

   *   *   *   *   *   *

  How distant seems our listlessness, our straining!
  Let's speak it o'er; we'll call it but our dreaming.
  We glide adown; empurpled day is waning;
    And far away our eddying path is gleaming.
Our hearts are very light, glad tones are calling.
We heed not, comrades, though the tide be falling!

  Our careless days are come, our toils surmounted;
    Nor think we longer of the frequent changing.
  Our store is all within, untold, uncounted;
    And we may sleep whilst those who slept are ranging.
Did we not well, O comrades, thus forestalling
The changeful tides—the rising, turning, falling?

IN REMEMBRANCE.

HOW shall I set a guard about my soul,
    To be at once a strong and sure defense !
    As on the long unnumbered years shall roll,
    How shall I shield each now unsullied sense ?

Of a perfection riv'ling human art,
    I'll place an image in some secret shrine ;
I have no dearer shrine than this pure heart,
    And it, receptive, makes that image—thine.

Then sweet remembrances,—thy rightful due,—
    Like precious incense round that cell shall wreathe ;
The measure of all worth shall be in hue
    Those harmonies that I have heard thee breathe.

How can my feet leave Honor's flowery path,
    Whilst, thus inshrin'd, thou hold'st that peerless place ?
How tread the weeds that Vice's broad way hath,
    In some base plain that thou wouldst scorn to grace ?

In baneful revelry should sense delight,
　Or tongue lend accent to the ribald jest,
I'd ponder, but thine eyes' reproachful blight—
　That stain might find no harbor in this breast.

Nor could this hand in harsh oppression fall
　(Should lowliness attain to high estate),
In soft repose 'twould stay, whilst I recall
　When it, of thine, had summ'd the gracious weight.

These are but idle thoughts—have ceased to live ;
　Such mean conceptions may not long abide.
Dishonor shall not win, I will not give,
　The sacristy thou keepest at my side.

Such is the guard I'll set about my soul,
　Since it so tends to be my soul's defense.
Come, long, unnumbered years ! whilst ye shall roll,
　A shield is set for each unsullied sense.

A THOUGHTLESS, BITTER WORD—TOO, HALF IN JEST.

 THOUGHTLESS, bitter word—too,
    half in jest,
  Above the sea-crests' breaking scarcely
    rang.
  But, then, it pierced the heart by mine
    loved best—
    Yea, pierced it with a needless, cruel
      pang.
A starting, as the varying colors rise;
  A dainty foot at toyings with the sand;
An instant's look of questioning, sad surprise;
  A failing gesture,—parted hand from hand.

MARJORIE.

LITTLE Marjorie, Marjorie mine,
    Why do you sink in the velvet grass?
Why are you so secret in your design?
    Come, show me that roguish face of
        thine.
Why, why is this? Little sunshine lass,
    On your dimpled cheek there's a glisten-
        ing tear;
    Your tremulous voice I can scarcely
        hear.

Of the fuschia you've broken the tender stalk,
    As you swept it by in your heedless chase!
There are fuschias yet by the garden walk,
    And myriads more in yon sunny space,
That come of a loftier, haughtier race.
Then brush the drops from your sparkling eyes:
I'll lead you to others of richer dyes.

Ah! *The loftier ones—you are careless of them!*
    And weeping again as your heart would break?
This was at best but an arrogant stem,
    And small is the worth of the life you take.
    But it loved you so for your own, own sake!
You granted it life by the pathway edge,
And grievingly, call it a broken pledge!

Little Marjorie, Marjorie mine,
  Soon to walk life's path with a measured pace,
Will your eyes ever grief like this inshrine,
  As you bow down a heart in some wayside place,
That dared to hope on by your thoughtless grace?
There's a dangerous light in your clearing eyes;
And your cheek with the crimson fuschia vies!

O, FLY THOSE MUSIC-BREATHING HALLS!

FLY those music-breathing halls,
    Mov'd by the soft, erotic flame!
To thee a sea of silver calls,
    And echoes but thy name.
Here for a time thy stay I would
    entreat,
  If thou wouldst hear the cadences
    that break
In lingering, piteous pleadings at my feet:
  She waits—she waits for thee and dear Love's
    sake!

Fly, fly on love's swift wings : for, list !
    A 'witching strain now floats above :
Too soon thy beauty shall be miss'd,—
    They'll say th' art fled with Love.
O, see for thee how thickly stars are spread !
    They wait to catch the plea yon wave shall make
As I have heard it here so often pled :
    She waits—she waits for thee and dear Love's sake !

    Then fly the halls of mirth and wine—
        Led forth in Love's persuasive name
    O, bend thine eager steps to mine—
        Led by Love's guiding flame !
Now thou art come, I fear I did deceive thee ;
    What cadences are theirs from me they take.
Then, dare my trembling hope in this believe thee,
    Fly, Love ! O, fly for her—for her dear sake !

LOVE'S INDEX.

O HAPPY, happy fate
    That brought me to the wood;
To the rustling, leafy bower
    Of my lady fair and good!
I'll come within its shade and wait—
    For soon she will appear.
I win or lose, this sunny hour,
    My lady coming near.

Some flow'ret to caress
    She stops the way beside.
O dear volume that she read—
    Let me from my ambush glide.
'Tis a poor lover in distress
    Upon its page that speaks.
O, let me learn then how he pled,
    Ere she her bower seeks!

I open and behold
    The all-absorbing text:
How the lover long laments—
    To my heart I lay it next.
'Tis there, where 'tis so sweetly told,
    My dew'd syringas rest;

And where long-waiting love consents
   My parting violet's pressed !

"I love but thee alone."
   O violet kiss the spot !
Let me to my ambush steal—
   That I gaze she'll know it not
Until I claim her for my own.
   She reads—O blushes rare !
I need no more my love conceal—
   My lady sees it there !

BEDOUIN ROBBER AND STEED.

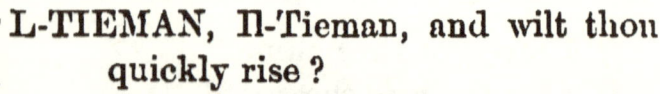L-TIEMAN, Il-Tieman, and wilt thou
quickly rise?
For see! the rosy-tinted morn flames
up the eastern skies.
I will offer up in Allah's name the
morning's glad devotion:
Before the burning sunbeams come
across the Indus ocean,
I'll grasp my scimitar and spear, my corselet round
me fling;
And then, my ardent Arab-steed, upon thy back
I'll spring!

Il-Tieman, Il-Tieman, whilst I slept into my dream
There came a vision of a spoil from Oman's pearly
stream.
My heart in secret rapture melts with its bliss and
happiness!
O princely steed, be ever true, as we o'er the
desert press!
For we may wrest a goodly gain ere the glowing
day is spent,
And spread it forth for wondering eyes in Mok-
allana's tent.

Il-Tieman, Il-Tieman, thou hast found me ever-kind;
So when thou hear'st my low command, then be fleeter than the wind.
I will breathe it in thine ear as I far away discover
The stranger's form,—nor by him seen. When dusky eve shall hover,
Then let him sink again to dream of founts and beds of flowers,
And his deep slumber shall be Death's—and his dreamings shall be ours.

Il-Tieman, Il-Tieman, thou dost bound and proudly neigh.
Fly from Ras-Fartak's rocky coast to Al-Akof's billowy way!
Frankincense fresh from balmy shores, and gems from Muscat's mart,—
If thou faint not, of these, my steed, thine be a gracious part!
On! on! thou ardent Arab-steed, upon thy back I spring!
Thy neck shall win a soft caress, thine ear with praises ring!

THE WATCHER.

STRANGER.

MAIDEN of the nightly shade,
   Why thy cheek so wan and pale
By the dews of night o'ersprayed?
   Gliding from the darkling vale,
     Shall Aurora of the dawn
     Ever greet thee wan and worn?

PHANTOM.

O, believe its pallid hue
   Finds within no answering chill;
And the pearly drops of dew
   Crystals are the airs distil!
     Are the hours so nearly gone,
     Envious Mother of the morn?

STRANGER.

Maiden, why thy couch forswear,
   And these lonely vigils keep?
Harmful gifts the dark winds bear.
   Haste thee to a peaceful sleep.
     Let thy night in dreams consume.
     Dian, watcher, doth illume!

PHANTOM.

Through the silvery festoons, knit,
   Turn thine earnest, upward gaze.
Note her, ever changing, flit,—
   So inconstantly she stays!
     Musing in expectant bliss,
     Speeds Endymion to kiss.

STRANGER.

Maiden, what imports it thee,
   Lustrous night and moonbeam's glance?
Why shouldst thou the watcher be
   Where wood-nymph and dryad dance?
     Of some treasure art bereft
     Near the shadowy mountain-cleft?

PHANTOM.

Where the last, long shadow dies,—
   Telling how the day is old,—
All-concealed my treasure lies
   In the secret, darksome wold.
     Fawn and wood-nymph may not know
     Where my heart is buried low!

STRANGER.

Maiden, hath the priceless heart
   Fled thy deeply stricken breast?

"Tis some phantom then thou art,
　Want'ning with thy nightly rest!
　　Choosing hours that noisome be
　　For thine errant misery.

PHANTOM.

Yes, 'twas priceless: yet I gave,
　Gave the heart that once was there.
Deep they laid them in the grave—
　Laid my heart and lover fair!
　　Ever nightly watch I keep
　　Where my heart and lover sleep!

SONNET.

DIDST ever thread, in the low Southern zone,
Some forest deep in sombre mosses clad,
Until the spirit sank, subdued and sad?
And, O what rapture! when, unthought, unknown,
To burst into some glade where sunbeam shone;
Where orange flower, and chaste magnolia bade
The wearied traveller stay, and, too, be glad,
And its endearing features make his own.
Thus, Edna, had my tortuous byway wound
Life's forestal and dusky depths, unlearned:
I sighed its wide expanse had set no bound,
Till to thy bright existence I had turned.
For its compare, for scope with graces crowned,
No sylvan scene this eye hath yet discerned.

DAVID AND ABSALOM.

("And the King commanded: Deal gently, for my sake, with the young man—even with Absalom.")

WHY doth high royalty forget its state,
    Cooling its feverish brow on frowning
        walls?
    Why doth it loiter by the ponderous
        gate?
    Why start anew as hurrying footstep
        falls?
And whence the apprehension that appalls
The kingly face of him in kingly guise,
Keeping his watch with fearful, constant eyes?

O monstrous deed! the fratricidal hand
    Now lifts to strike a father's form to earth.
Audacious pride has seen in dreams the wand
    Wrenched from the grasp of him who gave it
        birth,
    Thinking to gild a manhood's fruitless worth:
And now with foul intent, by folly led,
Seeks e'en the crown on the anointed head!

The mandate has gone forth: "Ye of the Lord
    For Israel's king, and Israel's kingdom, arm!"
And loyal breasts had flamed with true accord

To shield the monarch from the threatening
    harm;
Yet his great captain, Joab, valiant, calm,
Bears from those lips the trembling, low attest:
"Would ye might spare him of my house lov'd
    best!"

And Joab had gone forth with conquering
    power,
  Sinking ere noon-tide from the royal sight.
Time onward speeds and soon must come the
    hour
  To tell him if the battle went aright;
  And if the Lord yet tarried in his might.
For this it is he watches at the gate—
Forgetting self and dignity of state.

Yet comes no missive from the struggling field,
  And day o'er Palestine with eve is blending;
And who the victory claims yet unrevealed
  To him who feels within his breast contending
  Desire for vengeance on the oft-offending;
Then by a father's instinct deeper stirred
Almost forgives—forgetting how he erred.

But whence the cloud that in th' horizon shows?
  Surely no tempest mars the waning day?
Ever it moves, and with each instant grows:

It must be—'tis a herald comes his way
   Bringing good tidings of the ended fray !
He comes alone !   Auspicious tale expect,
How all goes well, and serried ranks unchecked.

Swiftly the runner leaps the fiery plain :
   Anon into the royal presence burst :
"Great tidings bring I, King, of thousands slain !
   And be rebellion ever thus accurst !
   And death to him whose arm is lifted first !"
One smile of triumph doth that face illume
And then a darkest aspect doth assume.

" Arise, thou panting herald, tell me, too,
   What tidings else beside the battle won.
Bring they my captive foe in chains to sue ?
   My captive foe ! stern fate ! my yet loved son
   Too early taught the honored way to shun :
Then let him come to meet a chastening hand,
And learn they rue who slight a king's command."

With awe the subject hears ; steps back apace,
   Viewing the face where mounting wrath held
     sway,
Wrought to its pitch by thought of how disgrace
   Must tarnish all the honor of that day,
   When conquering hosts in pomp and war's
     array,

Pass by their king with hymn and prayer devout,
With banners spread to joyous victor's shout.

He answering: "Israel's king, I saw him not;
   I waited but to see the conflict turn;
Thence speeded here in eager haste, and hot,
   Bringing such tidings as ye do but learn.
   And yet, methinks, so valiant son would spurn
Long to outlive the all-disastrous strife—
Setting no value to his hopeless life!"

The king hears not; his gaze afar is fixed
   Low, where the desert knits the flaming sky:
There, there, befoamed, the gate and sky betwixt,
   The Cushi comes! so swiftly comes he nigh,
   'Tis with an eaglet's wing he seems to fly;
Is near—is here—now in the presence kneels,
And gasping speaks—the tidings all reveals.

"Fierce was the battle, but the Lord prevailed!
   Far fled the foe, and scattered as the chaff
When by Sirocco's deadly breath assailed—
   So are thy foes before thy servant's wrath
   Blighted and whitening in rebellion's path!
And be it thus with all who scorn thy sway—
The sleep of Ephraim's wood—in death's decay!"

And David wept—his parent heart undone,
   "Would I had died, O Absalom, my son!"

SUNSHINE IN WINTER.

WINTER drear with Summer's smile;
    And we, joyous as the weather,
Listening to the waves that while
Rippling round the nestling isle,
    Pace the sands together.

Bound in none save Fancy's chain;
    'Neath the frowning castle's wall;
Questioning tokens from the main
As they come, to go again—
    And the shadows fall.

Sinks the sun to wonted rest;
    Bathes in warmth the chilling sea;
Silent we, each thought suppressed
As he nears the glowing west—
    Rich in imagery.

Ere the parting rays be told
    See them, lingering, softly lie
On my darling's brow of gold;
So, so nearly they enfold—
    Seeming loth to die.

List! the deep and sullen boom!
    'Tis the day's departing note.

In assurance of its doom,
Through the ever-gathering gloom
    Answering echoes float.

Longer linger ere I seek
    Where may wandering fancy be?
Lest untimely word I speak,
Bending low but touch the cheek—
    Breaks the reverie.

Shine, O mellow moon and mild!
    Be the homeward way pursued!
From the wintry day that smiled
Tenderly I lead the child—
    By its thought subdued.

GOLDEN HOURS.

What is a golden, golden hour—when day's departing beam
  Spreads crimson tints upon the cloud and gilds the mountain-crest;
When busy cares, that never sleep, fade in a misty dream;
When gladness gilds with darting beam the sorrows of the breast.
Pride stands abashed and deeply shamed, as, silently, the tongue
  Strives at the prompting of the heart with softest words to mould:
The sun shone yet upon thy wrath; the vesper-bell hath swung!
  That is a golden, golden hour departing beams enfold.

That is a golden, golden hour—when, on the desert drear,
  The Arab bids with fainting tones his dromedary kneel.
We drink this night, give Allah praise, from fountain deep and clear;
  Think not the morrow is at hand, but take the present weal!
Then the long, gleaming spear he grasps—aglow with many a ray,

Thrusts it o'erjoyed, with fervent prayer, deep
in the yielding sands.
On its gay pendants rest his eyes—the evening-
breezes play.
O golden, golden hour! he cries, and lifts the
bronzéd hands.

That is a golden, golden hour to Persia's happy
maid
Resting, her cheek upon her hand, above the
chalky cliff.
Round Oman's distant, hazy point, in ocean-
treasure laid,
Fades one with love in heart and arm to guide
his dancing skiff.
And well she knows he'll homeward turn ere
evening-shadows grow;
And well she'll watch until above the emerald-
wave he'll rise,
Then veil the cheek that would reflect the even-
ing's richest glow.
O golden, golden is that hour to Persian maiden's
eyes.

That is a golden, golden hour—and welcomed
with the eve,
When long-forgotten memories at Music's touch
awake;

When some, perchance, shall thrill with joy, and
 some, perchance, shall grieve,
 As on the ear the moving chords of harmony
  shall break.
O, when the gilded mountains lift beneath the
  crimson skies;
 When Music brings the absent near with her
  mysterious power;
When on the lilies of the field the longest shadow
  lies,
 The fairest of the hours hath come—the golden,
  golden hour.

LILY OF THE VALLEY.
(Return of Happiness.)

BECAUSE the world so coldly seemed to
 frown,
 He thought him in the darksome vale
  to hide;
 He gladly hastened there; he flung him
  down,
  And o'er his past and hopeless future
   sighed.
When O! he spies beside the grassy mound,
 Whose close confine restrain's the rill's dark
  thread,

A Lily of the Valley, too, had found
   With some intent this spot its sweets to shed.'

O emblem of the modest, pure, sincere!
   Art thou, too, strangely shrouded in some spell
That keeps thee from each blooming, fair compeer
   To be with me an exile to the dell?

The Lily of the Valley gently bowed,
   And gave from bounteous stores yet unconsumed.
The evening's zephyrs, hastening, went endowed
   And told afar the Lily yet perfumed.

My home deep in the valley hath been made,
   I uncomplaining : and its depths disclose
No answering tribute for my charms displayed—
   So in oblivion do my hours repose.

But in its solitude I bloom content,
   Since haply, as hath thine, some step may wend
Within its gloom, to find my beauty lent
   A quick retrieve where doubtings long contend.

O Lily of the Valley, with new aim
   Let me the turmoils of the world engage :
For true submission win thy fragrant name,
   That mine, as thine, some happiest hour
     presage.

SONNET.

THERE is an attribute of nameless gauge
    That Stoic may repel, cannot refute ;
    Philosophy essay, nor yet compute :
    Its virtue this—perennial. Through each age
    It curbs the savage and corrects the sage,
    (Whose inconcinnities, whose schemes astute
Corrupt their reasons), who esteem its fruit,
Which, if but plucked, matures at every stage.
Man may protest, – he never can despise
    The tempting flavor of its wholesome cheer :
    If now unblest, yet blessèd memories rise,
And rise to soothe, be whatso'er his sphere.
    Its home, the heart ; its beacon-fire, the eyes.
    Affection 'tis—that gift without compeer.

SONNET.

TO MYSIE.

(With the Rosebud.)

WITHIN thy hair
    This rosebud bear :
  Let it thy many dreamings
      share :
  Though it be now the young and
      glistening morn,
  Far up the heated day let it be
      borne.
If joyous, thou wilt have to spare ;
If sorrowing, tell thy secret care —
  But love it everywhere.

    In early night
    When glances bright
  Are sped to measures of delight,
Or mingled with a language low entoned,
Still be it on its favored seat enthroned.
  Then hours, by some mysterious right,
  Will, too, make pastime of their flight—
    Yet still its love invite.

    O whisper deep !
    When thou shalt sleep
Place it where angels watchings keep :

And that shall be—where 'tis reposing now
In ripening beauty—o'er thy blushful brow:
   And Night-winds, gazing as they sweep,
   Back to its unculled mates shall creep,
    And, envious, they shall weep.

ARSINOE.

[Cæsar brought Arsinoe to Rome; but, feeling compassion for the youthful princess, restored her to freedom.—*C. Com.*]

NEAR Rome. In its splendor the day is declining;
   They have led forth the fair Alexandrian maid:
   There she rests, like some statue, in pensive repining,
   Gazing deep down in Tivoli's foaming cascade.

They mercifully leave her; so, kindly befriending,
   They mercifully leave her, O unspeakable bliss!

There they leave her alone, with emotions con-
    tending;
  Nor could friendship devise kinder favor than
    this.

Above her are palaces, loftily towering
  In settings of glittering, unmatched colonnades;
But she heedeth them not—'tis in Tivoli's shower-
    ing
  That her soul seems enwrapt—'midst the bright
    rainbow-shades.

O'er its olive-clad rampart she bends in her dream-
    ing.
  Now some thought, for its recompense, wins a
    faint smile:
She hath seen in rude Tivoli's torrent, far-gleam-
    ing,
  Some resemblance that mocks her own languish-
    ing Nile.

Oh, unhappy transition! 'tis the tempest fore-
    telling
  Of tears and of sighings would she now might
    restrain;
For her thought on the deed of the morrow is
    dwelling,
  When, to grace the great triumph, she wears
    captive chain.

"Can he ever be thus? bears that heart no relent-
    ing?
  O, lead me to Cæsar; I will deign to implore:
He will weep in compassion, then, in pity consent-
    ing,
  Say, 'tis sweeter, far sweeter, than triumph in
    store."
    *   *   *   *   *   *

'Tis by Rome: and again as the day is declining,
  Far adown gushes Tivoli's foaming cascade.
And the one that dreams there, nor yet dreams of
    repining,
  Is the fair and unshamed Alexandrian maid.

SONNET.

WHEN on my brief existence I reflect,
    There seemeth made a safer path of joy
    Than idly resting, and the hours employ
With thought of past and future. I detect,
If I of dearest times past recollect,
    A shadow mingling in unasked alloy—
    'Tis that they are no more: and, if I toy
With those that yet await me, I suspect
Inquiet longings. But, if I secure
    In present hours do their good exact,
    My happiness is husband'd to endure;
And through my life I blessings may protract.
    By this, it seem'th to me, my hours assure
    Tranquillity the others surely lack'd.

THE MATINS BELL.

THE matins bell! awake, Sleeper, awake!
    Ere shall be heard
The first shrill signal of awakening bird,
    If thou hast err'd,
Out in the breaking morn thyself betake!

The matins bell! its music asks, Why doubt?
    It claims thy prayer.
The sky's aflame; dews gleam; 'neath it repair,
    And, trustful, bear
Midst earth's uplifted praise, thy prayer devout!

Its melodies have died; its tongue is still'd.
    Will't come again?
O pr'ythee, ere the sun gild spire and pane,
    Annul that stain;
And walk the day, thy soul with rapture fill'd!

EPIGRAM.

(Enforced absence.)

TO ———

AND can it be
    That Time conspires to stay his flight,
        And change for me,
    The blessings of the grateful light
    To that doth so resemble night?

    Ask some pale flower
Transplanted from the sun and dew,
    If sweet the hour?
No! No! 'twill cry, and weep anew.
I am that flower transposed from you.

SONNET.

COME, doubter, climb with me yon dizzy peak.
* * * * *
Thy gaze to'rd distant ocean first be bent :
Then nearer, scanning Nature's wide extent,
And what behold'st ? "Bright rivulets that eke
That ocean ; in woods of vocal tone seek
Happiest inmates ; of wondrous hue and scent
Bloom beds of flowers ; the fields, in colors blent,
Stretched to immensity. All good bespeak.
Some hand to deftly limn these do attest;
Too, of exhaustless skill ; these proof upbear
Of intellect untold. Whose hand else drest
The wave in silver, decked the hued parterre,
Or taught the rhythm the vocalist express'd?"
Such handiwork an All-Wise doth declare.

SONNET.

MINE ears drink in thy soul-outpouring lay,
    Thou love-lorn Nightingale! Methinks so, erst,
    Thy spell came o'er me; and, by memory nurs'd
    E'en till this hour. Over Sorrento's bay,
Wrapt in the mellowest tints of dying day,
    I hung with many musings. As 't did thirst
    For deepest sympathy thy plaintings burst
    Upon the evening's stillness, died away,
And left me marvelling. This summer-time
    Thou mad'st thy flight,—from Tasso's byways woo'd,—
    And tell'st thy sorrows in a sterner clime.
See, Philomela, earth again endued
    With much thou lov'st, with emerald fields and thyme:
    Then leave me not in more than solitude!

TO A SUNBEAM.

THOU trembling, molten beam
    Fresh from the fount of light!
Didst thou leap the mighty span,
    'Scape the chill and vaporous blight
To sink with uncorroded gleam
    Upon the slumbering earth;
And warm, again, her face so wan
    With hopes of spring-time birth?

Yet, tell me ere thou sink,
    And fetters thee enfold,
In those spaces unrevealed,
    In those fastnesses untold,
Dost thou of others else bethink
    In thine own bright attire?
And will they not there stay concealed
    If thou so soon expire?

Soft! sunbeam, thou shalt know
    What answer 'tis I crave,—
Now into my breast there came
    With the glow thy presence gave,
A hope; its beaming cheers me so
    I'd keep it long delayed;
But if none other bear thy name
    I fear it, too, may fade.

SONNET.

SPREAD o'er the South, of balmiest gales
    and bloom,
    There flowers a shrub that seems
        the veriest pledge
    Of beauteous constancy. If noxious
        sedge
    Encompass it, unmindful of the
        gloom
With the weird fen's it mingles its perfume.
    The traveller, fainting at the wayside's edge,
    Shall not forget it : o'er the frowning ledge
    It waves undaunted.   Nor did he presume
Who in a burning and remotest land
    Hailed it, "O pride of India !"   Oft for me,
    Pausing 'midst scenes all-lovely, memory
        spann'd
Eventful days and Nature's marquetry.
    And thou stood'st with me, Julia, and I plann'd
    What kinship bore this Pride of Inde to thee.

A TRIFLE IT WAS, AS LIGHT AS THE AIR.

A TRIFLE it was, as light as the air
    (And often and oft to recall it I've tried)
That lost me for ever a maiden fair,
    And that banished my promised bride.

In time it was even, and calm and still,—
    Would our passions might sleep in such deep content!
And we stood by the crystal, laughing rill,
    And our tones with its murmuring blent.

A trifle it was, as light as the air,—
    Ah, thou envious spirit—genius of Hate!
Why bring me so grievous a burden to bear?
    Why lay on my heart this leaden weight?

Of the years to come, and the years but flown,
    We had spoken and planned 'midst the starlight showers:
She seemed even dearer and more my own
    For the future seemingly ours.

O the sweet delight of those starlight dreams!
    What a mockery, too, of my ceaseless grief!

Then life flowed as tranquil as those soft beams
   That lodged in her odorous wreath.

Some trifle it was, as light as the air;
   But whether it was I or my own dear love
That changed life's bright day into night's despair
   Can she tell—or the stars above?

In a world so troubled it seems not right
   That fond lovers should part, and then not know why;
And that ties so strong from a cause so slight
   Should so weaken, and break—and die.

Some trifle it was, as light as the air
   That the zephyrs wafted from Egypta's strand
That tarried to toy with her fluttering hair,
   And her deepening blushes fann'd.

And they say she waited—grew faint at heart:
   But that day I was proud, and I thought her cold.
How I've sighed in vain, with miserly art,
   For the loss of that word untold!

Some trifle it was, as light as the air,
   Disturbing life's waters that rested as clear
As that crystalline lake called Leman, where
   The nightingale plainteth her fear.

I trust no shadow envelopes her hours ;
   And that life seems as fair as in those young
      days
When we walked through the almost silent bowers
   With the carpeting moonlight rays.

Some trifle it was, as light as the air—
   And by each repented ere it onward sped :—
To think that our lives should such shadows bear
   For a word—then a word unsaid !

MY MATE AND I.

WE come, my mate and I, belate ;
She wears a blossoming robe of state ;
   See, too, what wealth of bloom and
      health
      She's borrowed from each flower and
         elf :
      Released from chains we saw the light
Subdue the long, forbidding night.

O, it was then so radiant when
We heard the soul-outpouring wren :
" My joy be thine. O, come and twine
In gay festoons each spraying vine ;
The bellflower sways, by airs caressed ;
The eglantine in beauty's drest !"

In yonder glade we long delayed
To note the spoil the Hyblæan made.
O, life of bliss ! would mine were this,—
To every other care remiss,—
To rove forever, and to sip
The fragrance from the jessamine's lip.

We come, my mate and I, belate ;
We but the morrow's coming wait :
To call no need, for we shall speed,—
Our pathway 'll be the flowering mead,—
And shades shall even deeper lie
Ere homeward we, my mate and I.

THE BURIAL OF PIZARRO.

[Pizarro, after an unprecedented career of conquest and cruelty, met the fate he so richly merited—the assassin's dagger. The Cathedral of Lima (Ciudad de los Reges) was profaned by placing his body beneath the altar.]

CIUDAD de los Reges!
Stand, for the coming dead!
Onward the pageant rolls;
Deep-toned the minster tolls—
Stand ye who bled!

Ciudad de los Reges!
Gentle mother, bear it!
Gone is the blighting breath
From the bold scourge of Death—
Greet'st thou that spirit?

Ciudad de los Reges!
Oh, rather bid them cast
Him forth upon the earth
Whose heaven he made a dearth—
And sinks at last.

Ciudad de los Reges!
Bounteous treasure extolled,

He, all-athirst, allured
By dreams of gain, endured
All for our gold.

Ciudad de los Reges!
More merciful, less fell
Condor on yonder peak,
That from his fastness bleak
Swoops to the dell.

Ciudad de los Reges!
'Twas he—this son of Spain,
Who left in blackened track
Of iron hoof and rack
Unnumbered slain.

Ciudad de los Reges!
Thy Inca fetters bore
Till death unbound the chain,
Forged to the fearful strain
Of battle roar.

Ciudad de los Reges!
The father vainly kneel'd,
And mother, for the child
With piteous plea, and wild—
His heart was steeled.

Ciudad de los Reges!
The captive, too, implored—
To meet the smile of Death;
And curse with fainting breath
The name abhorred.

Ciudad de los Reges!
Bless'd mother, dost behold?
See! 'neath the holy nave,
And dome, and architrave,
They bear his mould.

Ciudad de los Reges!
What! sleep beside the saint
Whose hallowed life taught prayer?
Mingle his ashes there?
Their rest attaint?

Ciudad de los Reges!
Could then the vesper-peal,
Soothing the heart oppress'd
With ecstacy of rest,
Invite to kneel?

Ciudad de los Reges!
Languish would every tongue;
Pallid grow every brow;

Falter the rising vow
By anguish rung.

Ciudad de los Reges!
The 'bated cry didst hear?
"Back, menials! from his path—
Temp'st thou his sleeping wrath?
The dead is near!"

Ciudad de los Reges!
'Neath altar, echoing dome,
With Desolation's blade
Pizarro lowly laid!
O shaméd home!

FALTERING.

THE night, for promise spread,
   Lies darkly clouded:
The river's throbbing thread
   Flows deeply shrouded;
The vault with starry gems engrained,
The orb that in her beauty waned,
   In gloom are dying!
For night and flood, for orb and stars
   The winds are sighing.

*   *   *   *   *   *

Blest harbinger to save,
   The gales are veering!
From flood and starry nave
   The mists are clearing!
The orb with beauteous crescent dipp'd,
The dancing wavelets, silver-tipp'd,
   Are ever vieing.
Within my soul, O constancy,
   Dream not of dying!

SONNET.

AND had I planned thy steps, thou shouldst not go.
   Thou canst not soothe me with the fond deceit
   That in some hast'ning year our paths shall meet,
   And joy be sweeter for this parting woe
Than we have known—and else can never know.
   How sunless is thy smile's poor counterfeit!
   And fainter grows thy heart's tale-telling beat!
   This were not didst thou truly believe it so.
Well, I will hush this moaning heart and bruised,
   Nor picture summer days and thou not here.—
   Thou veil'st thine eyes, with manful tears suffused;
They say, when thou art gone thou'lt yet be near.
   Press, lightly press this hand as thou art us'd.
   Go, and remember thou art doubly dear.

SONNET.

TH' Assyrian monarch to uphold his throne,
   Set it on man, carved in war's dread array,
   Whose threatening aspect taught man to obey.
   That subject might not kindred awe disown,
The Persian his, of gold and glittering stone,
   Upbuilt in crouching form of beast of prey;
   And millions cried allegiance—felt dismay,
   And curs'd a pride to impious excess grown.
Beyond e'en these my Monarch's realm extends.
   My Master's state uprests on truth and love.
   O'er Asshur's grandeur desert-drift ascends,—
My Master's mounts th' empyrean heav'n above:
   O'er Elam's buried pomp his lion wends,—
   High soars my Master's gentle symbol-dove.

THE DREAMERS.

THIS child, in pleasant byways kept,
    Who sees life an unchanging May,
Forgot her mates ere sunbeam slept,
    And stole to me away.

Upon my kindly face and grave
    She glanced; and then upon my knee
Its rest her wearied head she gave,
    Half singing musingly.

She very often seeks me so,—
    I think because my face is grave:
She thinks I'm busied with the glow
    That silvers o'er the wave.

That on some orb my thought is set:
    So, struggling with its quaint conceit,
And busied so must needs forget
    The dreamer at my feet.

And so she sings, or murmurs o'er
    Some fancy I have given tone;
And murmurs it to love it more
    And make it more her own.

Than all the pleasant hours are
    There is an hour endeared to me—
When fancy leaves the wave and star
    For dreamer at my knee.

As thus: what devious paths—say fair—
    Of leagues untold its feet must tread!
Where shall it then, oppress'd with care,
    Thus lay its drooping head?

Will joy be her unbroken task
    (Such as to be these hours she finds),
And shall she but in sunshine bask
    Until her day declines?

Shall thought beneath this shining brow
    To images of beauty turn;
Or fan a flame that slumb'ring now
    Needs but a breath to burn?

Shall this fair hand, all zeal, engage
    To do the mandates of the heart;
And trace the ever-living page
    With Poesy's deathless art?

Or shall she, nameless, walk serene
    To shed abroad her woman's grace,
And bring contentment to the scene
    That's most a woman's place?

Would Heav'n for me—Heav'n stay the prayer!
'Twere best that thought no utt'rance gave;
'Twere best it now from dreamer bear
   Its dreaming to the wave.

ON CONTENTMENT.

HORACE: Ode 1, Book 3.

FROM him of low desires, uncared to rise,
   My soul revolts—from him I turn my eyes.
In silence listen, words unheard before,
   Ye youths and virgins, in your ears I pour.
Dread sovereigns o'er their subjects have control;
The kindred giants Jupiter extol,
Who with his nod the realm of Nature shakes,
And at whose glance the haughtiest Titan quakes.
Because, forsooth, this man in goodly row
Beholds in thrifty bloom his forests grow,

He lays his claim to nurture well the state:
The second protests—argues happier fate
From him within whom growing honor lies—
And his own worth and virtue loudly cries:
The third prefers his right—to long contend,
And boasts how myriads on his store depend.
But Fate, by all-impartial, fixéd laws,
Revolves the urn, each name unbiased draws.
How can that man his revelling hours enjoy
When hangs a point with purpose to destroy?
Can the Sicilian dainties relish bring
If o'er his brow the deadly dagger swing?
The tuneful lyre, the birds with soothing songs
Bring not the soft repose for which he longs.
Sleep to the peasant is a frequent guest,
And in his cottage loves to linger best:
If at the dawn he fly his barless doors,
At eve returns from Tempe's zephyred shores.
He with a competence, assur'd, possess'd,
Views the tempestuous sea—nor feels distress'd:
Arcturus in his wrathful fury sets,
Yet, in his heart no anxious doubt begets.
No vineyard he to tempt the ruthless hail;
No waving fields to droop before the gale;
No fruitful lands, with bounteous rains submerged,
Or else by rays from fiery planets scourged.
The swift finn'd tribes, that mighty waters range,

Behold the sea's foundations ever change :
And lordly man, disdainful of the land,
Sends down the chosen hirelings of his band ;
Yet apprehension ne'er forsakes his mind—
Care mounts the galley as the knight behind.
Since then, nor Phrygian block, nor gay attires,
Bring the contentment that my soul desires ;
Falernian vine, nor yet the Persian herb
Drown not the troublings that my hours disturb,
Shall I some lofty edifice erect,—
Since I the breath of envy must expect,—
With peerless column, modern taste adorned,
To hear my motive and its beauty scorned ?
Why give contentments of my Sabine Vale
For troubles oft possessed wealths entail ?

TO THALIARCHUS.

HORACE : Ode 9, Book 1.

BEHOLD Soracte clad in snows;
    The woods their leafy burdens cast;
Nor longer on the river flows—
    Frost's icy sharpness binds it fast.
Dispute the cold: pile high the blaz-
    ing boughs!
    O Thaliarchus, forget not your vows!
To cheer the coming youths afar
    The cheerful flames now upward twine.
Now, Thaliarchus, from the jar
    Pour out the generous, ruby wine.
Leave to the gods the vexious ills of life:
Think you no more must mingle in the strife.
    When winds the fervid ocean lash
        The vales in peace repose,
    The cypress and the aged ash
        Forget their coming woes.

To ask the morrow's hap forbear:
    Treasure this hour's unquestioned gain :—
Come, fill the cup,—nor think to share
    This draught with any future pain.
Joys of the young, O pleasant love and dances,
Abide with us, affrighting Time's mischances!

As on the mellow hours glide,
  The song and whisper oft repeat—
As in the hour of eventide
  Where Tiber laves our Martius' feet.
Give you no heed whence sweetest echo wends,—
Well with the mirth coy damsel's laughter blends.
  He'd seize some token from her arm,—
    Since eye in vain appeal'd,—
  What hour so fit to win a charm,
    Contending love would yield ?

TO QUINTIUS DELLIUS.

HORACE : Ode 3, Book 2.

O DELLIUS, repel not from your mind
That life, a dream, by you must be resigned.
Since this is so, your stores of joy expand
If you bethink its changings to withstand :
Do not shrink under Fortune's angry frown,—
The fruitful germ the husbandman cast down,

Which, lying hidden long in deepest gloom
Sprang forth, bore fruit, and gladdened with its
  bloom :
Nor yet, if viewing some unhoped result,
Think o'er your friend, less happy, to exult.
If nurturing sadness in remotest spot,
Or if to pleasure gods your hours allot
And lead you on to some inviting vale
With ease and wine your hours to regale,
While you recline within some grateful shade
The lofty pine and hoary poplar made,
And upward gaze as sunny cloudlets flit,
Or drink with rapture from the rivulet,
It is decreed, and these change not your fate—
Our hours the coming Sisters but await!
Bid slaves bring wine, perfumes of wondrous cost:
Not for a future let this day be lost.
Think, Dellius, depart, and soon, you must;
With you your treasures crumble not to dust.
O no! a longing and impatient heir
Makes them his waking and his sleeping care;
Surveys your villas and computes your groves,
And, penniless, expectant master roves.
It matters not if sprung from humblest race,
Whose ancestors no ancient records trace;
Nor yet could Argos claim thy noble sire—
From this fair scene you surely shall retire.

All are alike—unsheltered from the air;
And envious Pluto takes all for his share.
Remorseless Fates yet turn the restless wheel,
And Atropos yet grasps the severing steel
Too soon to cut the unresisting thread—
Forth from the breast the living spark hath fled!
Our destiny—born, linger here a while;
Embark with Charon for a long exile!

TO LICINIUS MURENA.

Horace : Ode 10, Book 2.

LICINIUS, life's ocean you may tempt,
    If you with prudence shall its paths
        explore.
    Guide not your bark where perils ne'er
        exempt,
    Nor yet, too timorous, press the threat-
        ening shore.

There is a path, in it you safely dwell—
    The placid current 'twixt the chafing strands;
The virtuous mean that shuns the hermit's cell,—
    Nor asks the palace envied greatness plans.

Th' aspiring pine met first the whirlwind's rage;
    The loftiest tower fell heaviest to the dust;
The tempests first opposing mounts engage,
    And deep within their forked lightnings thrust.

Discerning souls hope on whilst least they may,
    And banish hope when most they hold the right;
The taper pales its beams before the day,
    To shine the clearer at the hastening night.

Depressing Winter, with his hoary train,
    Great Jupiter sends forth—to soon recall;
Though luckless venture now deny you gain,
    No kindred fate your future's may befall.

Apollo lulls him with Euterpe's art,
    And drinks the transports of the modest Muse;
He flings aside his bow and cruel dart,
    Whilst in his breast her softest strains diffuse.

Bring forth your treasures when you need your friend;
    And happiest be when happiest thoughts avail.
'Twere best, Licinius, when the sails extend
    To watch for changings of the prosperous gale.

OUT ON THE MYSTIC SEA.

I.

OUT on the mystic sea
    Far, far from me ;
Down, down a sunset sea by zephyrs fann'd—
    Cradled to sleep.
When from the west the ruddy wavelets flow,
When at the eve the dying tintings glow,
    Thy trysting keep!
A cry, a wafture of a jewell'd hand—
    Out on the mystic sea
    Lost, lost to me!

II.

Over the mystic sea
    The false-rose came to me ;
A lowering, sunless sea it came across.
    Its bloom distill'd :
A love that's yet unpledg'd another woos !
In warmer strain than thine another sues !
    My heart was chill'd.
Back ! haste thee back, where mocking wavelets toss—
    Back to the moaning sea—
    Dark'ning to me !

III.

Up from the mystic sea
The heart's ease came to me;
A melting, sunset sea 'twas wafted o'er—
To lull my fears:
I breathe of thee to each departing wind;
I bathe this emblem to the waves consigned,
With love's own tears!
Than this, so gladdening missive never bore
The wondering sea—
Hark'ning to me.

TO GROSPHUS.

HORACE : Ode 16, Book 2.

O GROSPHUS, luckless is the man allur'd
To the wide Ægean, night's bright orb
    obscur'd.
With not one star the hidden course to
    mark
And promise safety to his tossing bark.
In such dark hours his heart one refuge
    knows—
To pray the gods for safety and repose.
   So, for repose the war-worn Thracian cries;
And 'tis for this the quivered Median sighs—
To find, alas! the gift is not secure,
Nor sword nor ransom yet its charms procure :
Nor princely bribe, nor deputy can bind
And banish tumult from the burdened mind.

   For peace that man a good foundation lays
Whom yet delights the board of humbler days.
For sordid wishes plenteous vaults to heap
Mar not his day, nor trespass on his sleep.
Why do we, by our arrogance misled,
Hoard up a store that others use instead ?
Why fly our climate, 'neath another sun
Begin a task, to vanish ere 'tis done ?

Whoever yet from country an exile
Persuaded Care to linger home the while?
He would not listen.   Care, consuming Care
Boards, too, his ship, and will his exile share:
Than stag more fleet, or yet the Orient's wind,
Care soon o'ertakes him, though delayed behind.
   A mind at rest, and joyful for its state,
Asks for no more, and thanks the watchful Fate.
In patience walks the fiery hours of trial;
And views correction with a placid smile;
And feels how true it is, how oft express'd
That not with life is man completely bless'd.
Achilles died—nor yet for death mature;
Tithonus lived—but youth could not endure;
And time may me from countless ills defend,
And yet to you no courtesies extend.
For, now, towards you the waves of fortune flow—
Flocks loudly bleat, Sicilian heifers low;
Your steeds in costly trappings swiftly fly;
And vestured you in robes of Tyrian dye.
But Fate my arts have never yet suborned—
She found me lowly, keeps me unadorned.
Yet this she grants, more prized than robe of
         down,—
A secret spurning for the rustic's frown;
And this besides,—than this I would not choose,—
A silent hour with the Grecian Muse.

EXQUISITE DRAPERIES HANGING IN THE WEST.

(JUNE THE TWENTY-SECOND.)

EXQUISITE draperies hanging in the west,
Of purple, yellow, and the warmest red.
Long journeyed he who burning sank to rest.
"Tell me, what day is this so sweetly dies?
Comes such another? Too, too soon 'tis sped!"
In answer whisper, whilst the soft, dark eyes
Break from the colorings of the western skies,
"Year's longest, fairest, happiest day is dead."

THE HOURS.

THERE is an all-enrapturing hour—
    When morn (the sea and sky ascending
Since rousing from his Orient bower)
    With a more constant hue seems blending.
The ruddy hour is youth—when joy
    At childhood's every prayer comes thronging.
The change—when ripening years alloy
    With promise of a worthier longing.

There is an hour—the full noon hour—
    With myriad forms the ocean whit'ning :
That laugh at Tempest's threatening power—
    Their present toil some future bright'ning.
The scene responds to life : the forms
    At hazard with life's heartless ocean
Are manhood's—heedless of the storms,
    And ardent for the wild commotion.

There is an hour—a silent hour—
    That's sacred to the evening's shading.
This sunbeam sighs that shadows lower ;
    With true submission this is fading.

The too soon hour is age; regrets
  Mayhap enfold with ceaseless thronging.
The change—when drooping age forgets
  Its nearest for a worthier longing.

ON HIS OWN WORKS.

HORACE: Ode 30, Book 3.

I CROWN my finished monument.
It shall endure though long be spent
The Northwind's unavailing power,
And the insidious, wastful shower;
Nor Years in unrelaxing might,
Nor Seasons in recurrent flight
Cast it with their destroying hands
To mingle with the ruthless sands.
I shall not die; my better part
Calls not for Libitina's art.
While priest and vestal shall ascend
The Capitol, so long contend
Successive ages to prolong
Praises to my melodious song.

Where Aufidus with cheerful mirth
('Twas thus he murmured at my birth),
Leaps o'er the plain with rapid stride;
Where Daunus' thrifty sons reside
Shall it be said: By minstrel tongue
Were softer measures never sung!
In wonderment that my refrain
Can woo the coy Æolic strain.
Melpomene! the praise be thine,
Since I may wear the Delphic vine.

I AM DYING, EGYPT, DYING.

(Antony and Cleopatra.)

I AM dying, Egypt, dying!
Bend thee lowly to the sand;
Soothe me with thy loving hand.
(Stay, O Death, thou all-denying!)
Of the thousand fond caresses,
  This, thy last, the damp brow presses.

Dark'ning, Egypt, ever dark'ning!
Hast thou then no bitter tears—

Ere the hastening shadow nears?
Nearer, nearer to my hark'ning!
Where my fainting sense shall hear it
Pour the fulness of thy spirit.

Fading, Egypt, day is fading!
Is it that Death's shadow creeps,
That thy stricken spirit weeps?
Is thy torment in upbraiding,
That the love of which thou gavest
Brought dishonor to a bravest?

I am dying, Egypt, dying!
Quick! the death-repulsing wine.
Pledge, by all that love of thine,
When thou seest me basely lying
Thou wilt then, repelling sorrow,
Thought of vanished greatness borrow.

SONNET.

AT times, on day of fervid Summer's reign,—
When in sore anguish droop'd each thirsting plant
As quite despairing,—then, behold, aslant
The long drawn beams, that for no instant wane
Until their fount yon glowing verge attain,
Fall tiny streamlets, whose rich graces grant
Reviving draughts for which the full fields pant,
And new existence to the velvet plain.
O healthful influence of the bursting shower—
Scarce dim the sunshine, bring the earth relief,
Lend each beam beauty, verdure darker green!
Must cloud hang o'er thee thus I'd have it lower:
To thine own blessing spend its wholesome grief—
And give the freshness of the sunshower scene.

TO THE ROMAN PEOPLE ABOUT TO ENGAGE IN CIVIL WAR.

HORACE; Ode 7 of the Book of the Epodes.

WHY, O impious men, this haste?
Go ye forth again to waste
   Store of Roman blood?
Have ye not too oft bedewed
Field and ocean's solitude
   With a crimson flood?

Shame upon ye that ye turn
Not where men of Carthage spurn
   That ye long delay!
That yon Briton yet disdains
Power of legion, nor in chains
   Treads your sacred way.

Will ye give the Parthian joy?
That ye thus your swords employ
   Thrills him with delight:
See! he cries, our haughty foe
Deals himself the deadly blow—
   Topples in his might!

Think ye! in the brutish race
Did ye ever, watchful, trace
  Deed like this defined?
Wolf and lion for the mate
Show compassion—spend their hate
  On aggressive kind.

Give the answer, nor withhold:
If by madness, crime controll'd
  Or the restive arm?
All are silent; faces pale
Ere the guilty soul prevail—
  Urging on to harm!

By a stern fatality,
Romans, must this ever be!
  So, ye stand dismay'd!
'Twas for this our Remus sank;
That the earth a torrent drank
  Fresh from brother's blade!

HYMN.

I.

MY Lord, my guard, my watcher, and my guide,
   Thou ever present, ever faithful friend,
   Than thee what refuge have I else beside?
   Yet I've no merit that can me commend.

II.

Doth not thy love from love like mine revolt?
   I give thee chiding when I owe thee praise:
Though grieved, thou striv'st to mend each harmful fault.
   I wound thee in a thousand needless ways.

III.

I see thy wondrous power. I know the hand
   That set the earth and heavens must be divine.
The glittering hosts wheel on at thy command;
   No will rebellious to thy will—save mine.

IV.

The deep-stirred ocean symbols forth thy wrath;
   And thunders but reverberate thy tone;
Thy glance would be the lightning's withering
    path:
   And all revere thee—all save I alone.

V.

Thy generous gifts unstintedly are poured;
   I them at morning, noon and eve expect.
I take these gifts— and pass thee unadored.
   Canst thou spare me and this, too, recollect?

VI.

Down, down, sad soul, in thy humility!
   A barren homage 'tis thou pay'st at best.
How can He more extend his gifts to me?
   Sink, head, upon the now tormented breast!

ALTHÆA AND MARIGOLD.

O REGAL, royal Marigold,
My secret I may not unfold!
When came the far-outrunning
    beams
I broke me from my drowsy dreams;
I sought thee—of the dawning hour
The proudest and the queenliest
    flower.

O heartless, heartless Marigold,
My dream of dreams shall not be told!

Thy blooming mates have called in vain:
I brushed them by in quick disdain.
Stay! stay! cries sweetest Mignonette,
Why these surpassing charms forget?
While Marjoram, in arts unlearned,
Her thought in artless blushes burned:
Nay! echoed Amaryllis, nay!
Not from my splendor turn away!

And I: My eyes the dewy glance
Of Marigold shall soon entrance!
O comrades of the summer field,
Shall it the rapturous answer yield?
In semblance hers, too, doth there dwell
A heart to love her lover well?
They mocked me; vowed thee, Marigold,
What I have found thee—cruel, cold!

SONNET : FOR JANUARY.

THE disenthralled and uncorrupted band
   Sweeps down from chilling realms.
      Its store expends
   In one symphonious whole.   The
      prospect blends :
   And lo ! the panoply by Grandeur
      plann'd,
With moor reluctant to the swain's demand,
   In purity harmoniously lends
   An unmatched, surfaced tablet, that contends
   To take the tracings of the Master-hand.
And thus the soul, by nobler, pure desires
   Its lavish or its meaner dress conceals
   By fairer aspect : and, new born, aspires
To purposes this fresh emotion yields.
   And all bewonder'd muses past attires—
   And wondering, germs of excellence reveals.

UNRECONCILED.

’TWAS in the eventide
    She, wistful, ever tried
To whisper what they said might
    be my name.
    They led me to her side
With blanched face and flying
    step. I came—
To see her smile, and fold a lifeless frame,
    And be my name denied.

    It was a cruel blow.
    And when I told them so,
They sadly smiled, and said, Mayhap tis well.
    But then how could *they* know?
I, in fierce anguish turning, bade them tell
How all-progressive time could break the spell
    Of my immortal woe.

    ’Tis well!—I’ll not believe!
    Such words shall never weave
Attunèd chords to suit my heart’s refrain.
    Would that I might conceive
The sun to sink forever ’neath yon plain,—
So careless am I if he rise again,
    So deeply, deeply grieve!

SONNET.

(To ——, with the Odes of Pindar.)

THE Macedonian prince, his rage to sate,
    Gave up the Cadmean town to dreadful flame;
    And thought by horrid act his foe to tame
    And feed base pride; unwitting, that, innate,
In lowly hovel, so on throne of state
    There is a power in a worthy name.
    Such now before the monarch's reason came—
    And mercy show'd to grace his deed of hate.
Whose wrought revulsion, and could pity urge?
    It was our poet's—him thou'lt now peruse.
    Oft in my bosom waves of scorning surge,—
Since men the evil, not the better choose,—
    To sink anon; in kindlier aspect merge:
    'Tis when upon thine honored name I muse.

INVOCATION.

POLHYMNIA, sweet, meditative Muse,
Wilt thou forsake me? wilt thou, then, refuse
To fan within this breast the subtle flame
With thy quick breath? O rash, unfruitful aim—
To sweep the strings when thou art far away,
Hoping for strains responsive to the lay!
Thou art more near: in night's deep, silent hour
Choosing to contemplate. Behold, thy power
The flickering flame awaits! Thou drawest near,
And poesy, exultant, quells her fear!
O, let thine own soft presence, 'till the dawn
Presents the steeded chariot of the morn,
Linger about me: lest it come, undimm'd,
To note my lyre unstrung—my theme unhymn'd.

LINES.

"The sense of death is most in apprehension." M. for M.

WHEN wayworn and o'ertask'd, 'tis well for thee
To cast thy frame on downiest of beds
While wafts the spirit o'er oblivion's sea,
Or takes some path which it, delighted, treads.
Did memory grieve—belike the grief's forgot;
Thy hope high winging—yet it upward dares;
If thou art humblest—now it frets thee not;
And here is rest for him of weightiest cares.
Wouldst thou withhold from sleep's encircling arms
Because it sought thee with unpromised date?
Would wakefulness, environed by its harms,
Not seem to thee by far a sterner fate?
Since death's a dateless sleep, we need not dread
The dear employments of the happier dead.

SONG.

[Knight of the Twelfth Century.]

MY king is proud: his fleur-de-lis
   Floats from his foeman's loftiest wall.
Saint Louis is the brimming pledge
   In yon ancestral hall.

My steed is proud: he gladly neighs;
   His neck of gold in fealty curves;
He bears to list of knightly fray
   The mailèd knight he serves.

My heart is proud: for Beauty's sake
   I set this day a trusty lance.
I die; or on my breast I wear
   The loveliest flower of France.

THE BATTLER.

THE Battler gazed the table round,
    Then fell his heavy hand:
Now by the tomb and by the cross
    The Moor shall leave the land:
I nightly vow it in my dreams;
    I swear it when I waken:
The infidel shall fly this realm—
    Toledo town be taken!

Then brighter grew each liegeman's eye,
    And darker grew each frown,
As, breathing forth his haughty threat,
    The Battler sat him down.
Dead silence reigned within the hall,
    As filled each ruby cup,
Then right, then left, each grandee gazed,
    And to his feet sprang up.

Now in the name of our Castile,
    Now by thy kingly name,
It was for this with ringing hoof
    My fiery charger came!
If thou speak'st truth, by plume and spur,
    The dusky Moor shall rue
The hour he spurned his desert home
    And cross'd yon sea of blue!

THE BATTLER.

Deep, deep they drink : the Battler now
    Pushed far his chair of oak
To clasp with iron clasp each hand,—
    'Twas thus again he spoke :
Ere set of sun at morrow eve
    A puissant horde shall near ;
They come to greet Toledo town
    With banner, strain, and spear.

Out boldly spoke Gallicia's son :
    From snowy fastness, I :
Than not to draw a freeman's breath
    'Twere better far to die !
We are a numbered band and brave,
    Nor long may stay the shock,
But let us keep at morrow eve
    Toledo's guardian rock !

'Tis well ! the Battler cries, 'tis death !
    Get each man to his shrine,
And ask, with fervid prayer, a charm—
    As I'll away to mine :
I'll bid my charger to it straight—
    Deep in the wood confin'd.
I speed a score of leagues this night
    Of beating rain and wind !

The vizor hides the burning eye;
    He turns upon his heel—
Across the court and swinging bridge
    Is heard the ringing steel.
He flies; and all unreined he knows,—
    That gallant steed he rides!
He'll bear the Battler to his shrine
    With long and trusty strides.

On, on (so hours) 'neath roaring top
    Of leaf, and sighing bough,—
That untired steed has checked his flight—
    The shrine's before him now.
The Battler's hand's upon the door:
    What is't his eyes shall greet,
That gives his eyes a softer light,
    His heart a quicker beat?

The Battler's little daughter 'tis,
    Deep hidden in the wold;
A menial's watchful care is she,
    With mother-care untold.
He knows that she must sweetly sleep, —
    As when he's gazed before
To lend his arm that ardent strength,
    A deadlier name to war.

With folded arm yet ponders he
   Where long the lashes rest ;
Bends low to meet the rising prayer
   The parted lips express'd :
"Jesu, when in the lonely night
   The Battler rides afar
That harm befall him not, I pray
   He be as angels are."

A treacherous tear from Battler's eye,
   The rounded cheek alarms ;
An instant—and that childish form
   Sways in the warrior's arms :
    *   *   *   *   *   *
Through darkling wood, through bridgeless stream
   Cries out a form of steel :
Come forth with Battler, comrades all,
   We conquer for Castile !

LAKE AND WILD-FOWL.

IGH in the leaden skies,
Dark'ning the icing lake,
See, see the wild-fowl rise !
Knowest thou where 'tis he flies ?
Why he should me forsake ?

    I have seen, I have seen down the lowering sky,
White messengers flit on the blasts that awake ;
And I go where the far-darting sunbeams yet lie,
On the berrying brier and the ripening brake.

    List to the cry he gave !
    Ere down the gale he wings,
    Ere in the cloud he lave.
    Soaring above the wave,
    What is the dirge he sings ?

Fare ye well, fare ye well, thou wert dear to my heart :
Then I laved in your ripples and deep, flowing springs,—
Now cold art thou grown : I in sadness depart
For my everglade home—where the trailing moss clings.

High in the leaden skies,
Dark'ning the icing lake,
See my Inconstant rise!
Care I not where he flies,
So he can me forsake.

THE BATTLE-FIELD.

(Gettysburg.)

I WALKED the battle-field,—a smiling plain
   With Autumn's many tints now all aglow,—
Where lay the anguished, the unnumbered slain—
   Where spread the awful pageantry of woe.

A hero of the strife, with 'bated breath,
   Told of the days of mighty fears and hopes:
With finger traced the carnival of Death,
   Held on the tablet of those hills and slopes.

It is a goodly scene ; the eye delights
    To rove from plain to distant wooded side.
It finds no foeman on the misty heights,
    Whence burst the flaming, all-destroying tide.

And, as along the crests and vales we strayed,
    Whence grew a grateful Nation's fond renown,
Spoke of the nameless dead—in deeds array'd :
    Or paused upon the hill's encircled crown.

And so they perished not : their honored fates,
    Graved on the shaft, is that of battle-stain.
The stainless marble to a world relates,
    Of honored dead that have not died in vain.

LINES.

MINSTREL, stay! thou shouldst be done:
   On the hearth cold lie the embers.
Believe thy gentle heart hath won,
   Believe the gentle heart remembers.
Cease; thy wearied hand must fall;
   It is weary with thy dreaming.
Cease; the shadows on the wall
   Show that day will soon be gleaming.
From thy musing turn away.
   Break the spell that doth enchain thee:
For thy lamp of flickering ray
   With its paleness doth instain thee.
Believe thy spirit's joyous bound
   Will another's move to gladness;
Believe thy spirit's softer sound
   Will another's move to sadness.

Minstrel, stay! let not thy cheek
   Tell the fear thou shouldst be keeping:
Nor thy traceried pages speak
   Of a silent minstrel weeping.
Minstrel, stay! thou shouldst be done;
   On the hearth cold lie the embers:
Believe thy gentle heart hath won,
   Believe the gentle heart remembers.

FINIS.

www.ingramcontent.com/pod-product-compliance
Lightning Source LLC
Chambersburg PA
CBHW021803230426
43669CB00008B/621